Settle to Carlisle

Settle to Carlisle
A Railway Over the Pennines

by W. R. Mitchell and David Joy

Dalesman Books
1987

CARLISLE
CUMWHINTON
SCOTBY
COTEHILL
ARMATHWAITE
LAZONBY & KIRKOSWALD
L.N.W.R.
M.R.
LITTLE SALKELD
LANGWATHBY
PENRITH
CULGAITH
NEW BIGGIN
LONG MARTON
N.E. Closed
APPLEBY
ORMSIDE
CROSBY GARRETT
KIRKBY STEPHEN
TEBAY
N.E. Closed
Ais Gill
GARSDALE
M.R. Closed
N.E
DENT
HAWES
L.N.W.
RIBBLEHEAD
HORTON
Closed
M.R
M.R.
SETTLE

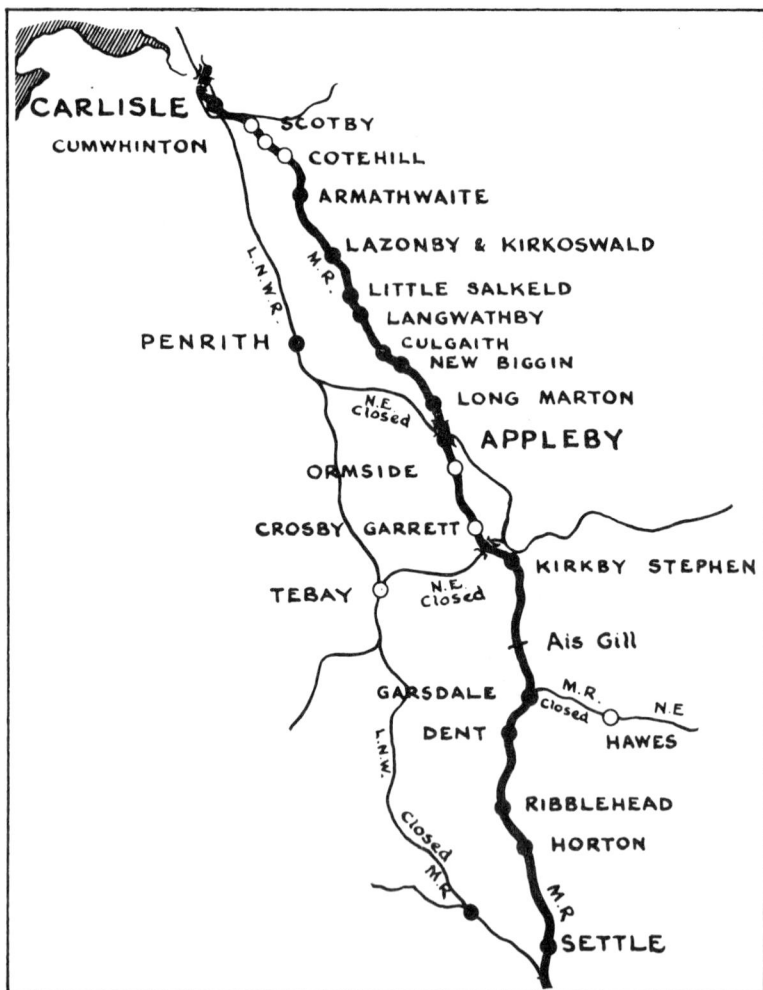

The Dalesman Publishing Company Ltd.,
Clapham, via Lancaster, LA2 8EB
First published (as Settle - Carlisle Railway) 1966
This Edition 1987
© W. R. Mitchell and David Joy, 1987
ISBN: 0 85206 893 X

Printed in Great Britain by
Smiths of Bradford, Bradford, England.

Contents

Illustrations

Our cover picture: 4–6–0 No. 850 *Lord Nelson* heads the 'Cumbrian Mountain Express' out of Garsdale (J. Winkley). Map by E. Gower. Etchings from the books of Frederick S. Williams: title page, 4, 14, 28, 31, 36, 63, 67, 68. Other drawings: J. A. Marshall, 2. E. Heeley, 27. E. Gower, half title page, 25. All uncredited photographs by W. R. Mitchell.

Preface

WHEN this book was first published in 1966 the Settle – Carlisle railway was but a neglected backwater. Trains pounded their way over the high fells accompanied not by mass clicking of camera shutters but merely the odd bleating of sheep or crying of lapwings. England's highest and most scenic main line languished largely unrecognised.

Twenty-one years later – and with over 30,000 copies of our book sold – the Settle & Carlisle now provides media fodder on a massive scale. Saving the line from closure has ceased to be merely the avowed aim of railway enthusiasts and has instead become a national cause. A quite unparalleled wave of opposition has in true British fashion seen entrenched positions assumed and battle lines drawn.

These words are being written at the same time as the Transport Secretary considers the massive report submitted to him by the Transport Users' Consultative Committees. Weighing-in at 22 kilos, it 'strongly and emphatically' recommends against closure. Time and politics will tell if this plea is to be heeded and the line reprieved, or if it will simply be left to decay into what would be Britain's longest ancient monument.

W. R. Mitchell and David Joy
March 1987

An Introduction

WHAT IS IT about the Settle–Carlisle railway that stirs the interest of so many people – that prompts an enthusiasm verging on mania in a few happy sufferers from what has become known as Settle-Carlislitis? It was natural, when the line was first opened over a century ago, for people to gather in excited knots at vantage points along the route, to watch the passing trains.

A parson in Mallerstang wrote with poetic feeling of the nightly vigils that were popular – of the thrill of seeing a Scotch express, firebox aglow, rush screaming by. John Delaney, who made a fortune out of quarrying in North Ribblesdale, and who lived near the railway, timed the regular trains and was known to rise from his bed and rouse the sleeping household if an express train was late in passing!

The Settle–Carlisle has retained its romance, even into the shabby modern period, when most of the stations are closed, and the gloss has gone from many of its fitments. Reminding us of Victorian endeavour on the grand scale, the railway still has a power to excite us. When a 'steam special' is due, there may be upwards of 1,000 photographers standing by those stretches of the line where it crosses the wilderness, between North Ribblesdale and the Eden Valley.

For 10 years, diesels-only operated on the 72-mile long railway, for British Railways did not want steam locomotives to pass under its precious new electric wires near Carlisle. Then, in 1978, a steam-hauled train returned. A gala atmosphere was detected at Ribblehead, despite the atrocious weather, with mist and driving snow. We saw a plume of smoke, a shade denser than the mist, and *The Green Arrow* appeared, speeding towards the viaduct, being little more than a smudge against the swirling vapour. It was enough to alleviate in the keenest observers yet another attack of Settle-Carlislitis.

This is clearly no ordinary line. A first-class rail system extends across the Pennines. Part of its appeal is in the devil-may-care attitude adopted by the engineers who faced rough and mountainous terrain. One Victorian engineer compared the profile of the Settle–Carlisle to a whale 'lying on its belly, with its nose in

Settle, its tail at Carlisle.' This whale measures 22 miles from nose to crown of head, and a further 50 miles from here to the tip of the tail! Two-thirds of the Settle–Carlisle is in the county of Cumbria, and over the bustling years a preponderance of Carlisle men have worked its trains.

There are currently many speed limits on the line because of the condition of the track, with a 30 m.p.h. 'slack' on traffic using the now single-line over Ribblehead viaduct. A further restriction occurs at British Gypsum, in the Eden Valley, where trains must not exceed 30 m.p.h. The section near the works has for long been called Magee's Slack, with old miners claiming that here the famous line is supported by pit props.

The footplate men who thrashed the trains over the first gruelling 22 miles of the 'Carlisle road' called it The Long Drag. A Carlisle fireman told me it was short and sharp; the Longer Drag from Edenvale to Aisgill often demanded more effort, 'blood for money', indeed. When at night the perspiring firemen of a southward-bound locomotive saw the glow of the signal at Aisgill, he knew his spell of really hard effort was almost over.

A story is related of a fireman, trained in the flat York area, who came for a spell to the Settle–Carlisle. The veteran driver on one journey was perturbed at the approach of The Long Drag to see that the fire was quite low, and he mentioned this to his companion, who was offended: he knew the job! As the train passed the Craven Quarry near Langcliffe, the driver beckoned to the fireman, and directed his attention to the top of the chimney at the Hoffman kiln. That chimney was over 200 feet high. The driver patiently remarked that in next to no time the train would be at Aisgill, at the same height as the chimney top. The fireman looked again – then shovelled furiously.

The line was built by the Midland in a short, feverish spell of activity, and at a cost of nearly £3,500,000 – an enormous sum when set against the economic conditions of the 1870s, and some 50 per cent over the budgetted figure. The railway took to the hills, but was not daunted by them. The climb from Settle Junction to Aisgill (1,169 feet) was planned with a ruling gradient of 1 in 100, which means that the engineers had to angle the line from its very beginning, to gain no less than 740 feet. 'This line', O. S. Nock has noted, 'is the only mountain railway in the world which was built for express trains.'

The fast, through, all-weather route to Scotland was a triumph over the many quirks of local topography. The straightest possible route was selected. If the engineers encountered a hill, they drove a tunnel through it. When a bluff was reached, a cutting was made. Every awkward valley was exalted by having a viaduct slung across it. Several million cubic yards of material were poured into quaking bogs. To take the line across the watershed at Aisgill with a continuous comfortable gradient, sections of the line were laid on ledges cut from lonely fellsides.

When the work was done, a newspaper observed: 'Perhaps nowhere in the kingdom has nature placed such gigantic obstacles in the way of the railway engineers as have been encountered over the 72 miles lying between Settle and Carlisle.' To other writers, the awesome Pennine weather was of paramount interest. In 1874, one who toured the still incompleted works, and who mentioned unfavourable comments by some at the slow rate of progress, declared: 'Let them go over it in the drenching rain of October . . . wade through mire, clay and water, and see the slurry spreading far beyond the company's boundaries, embankments cracking and slipping away from the metals, and add to these difficulties the cuttings through boulder clay, and rocks of excessive hardness, the roving habits of the workmen and the wild and inhospitable district through which it passes, and then the wonder will not be that the works are incomplete, but at the possibility of completing them at all.'

Twenty large viaducts, 14 tunnels, no sharp bends: here was an engineering triumph by a company which could list 'pride' among its assets. The stations that appeared in the dales and on the fellsides were substantial buildings, faced with stone, and with steeply-pitched roofs, in a style that was to be termed 'Midland Gothic'. At the southern end of the line, considerable quantities of stone were brought in from the quarries of Bradford, or local material, including limestone, was employed. The Eden Valley sprouted stations fashioned from the glowing rose-red sandstone of that region. The railway-builders were quick to use local material where it was suitable, and – for example – a particularly hard rock taken from Anley Cutting was used for the construction of local bridges.

Some of the Pennine rainfall was tapped for use in the locomotives and, quite apart from the strategically-placed water cranes there were, near Garsdale, the highest water troughs in the world, fed by a 40,000 gallon tower which, for a time, was steam-heated as a precaution against frost. This was installed in 1907. Water from a stream was held in a dam on the fellside. A man who worked on that dam observed that the foreman attempted to save the Midland money by using rather less concrete than specified. The result was that when the stream was directed back into the area of the dam, it leaked like a colander, and had to be made again!

Despite its massive works, the Settle–Carlisle does not dominate its setting. If you follow the old Coal Road, now tarmacadamed, between the stations of Garsdale and Dent, you will see the famous line and also its wild setting. Pennine giants – including Ingleborough, Whernside and Wild Boar Fell – give added character to the skyline. The road extends by Shaking Moss to an elevation of 1,761 feet. You may watch a Garsdale farmer clip sheep in crofts beside the road, and listen to the low, sad whistle of a golden plover, a sound reaching you across a succession of solitudes. Then descend towards the valley of the upper Dee, and observe a white-painted building gleaming like a mirage against a landscape in shadow. This is the stationmaster's house, now in private hands – the first evidence of the nearness of Dent station which, at 1,100 feet above sea level, is the highest railway station in England. Old snow fences, composed of upreared sleepers, accentuate the sense of remoteness.

From Dent station, the eye traces the line of the railway towards Blea Moor. Into view come the viaducts of Arten Gill and Dent Head, like Victorian cobwebs spanning the gills. The toot of a steam locomotive is heard as a 'steam special' ticks off the miles to Aisgill. White smoke issues from Blea Moor Tunnel. A trail of smoke, kept low by a Pennine breeze, establishes the position of the train as it nears Dent station. The fells are on such a scale that the train looks like a toy.

James Allport, the Midland's general manager, was not a squeamish man, for he was known as the 'Bismark of Railway Politics'. Yet after visiting the high hills where the line was to go, he asserted: 'I shall never forget, as long as I live, the difficulties surrounding the undertaking . . . We walked over the greater part of the line from Settle to Carlisle, and we found it comparatively easy sailing till we got to that terrible place, Blea Moor.'

The story of how the Settle–Carlisle came into being has been told in considerable detail. Here is a brief summary. During the 1860s, the Midland was a powerful company intent on expansion to all parts of Britain. In its northward progress, it infiltrated the Leeds and Bradford Railway, which had metals up to Skipton, and the 'Little' North Western Railway on which trains could be operated as far as Ingleton. It was here that the Midland had a setback. The Ingleton–Lowgill line, a branch of the mighty Lancaster–Carlisle, was controlled by a serious rival, the London and North-Western. To gain access to Scotland for its goods and passengers, the Midland had to hand them over at Ingleton; they were not given a high priority.

Allport noted: 'It is a very rare thing for me to go down to Carlisle without being turned out twice. I have seen 12 or 15 passengers turned out at Ingleton, and the same number at Tebay. Then, although some of the largest towns in England are on the Midland system, there is no through carriage to Edinburgh, unless we occasionally have a family down, and then we make a special arrangement and apply for a special carriage to go through. We have applied in vain for through carriages for Scotland . . . I have frequently had letters from passengers complaining that they could not get booked through. I have sent letters to Mr Johnson from passengers requiring to come to Derby when booking at Glasgow, and they have been told to go by way of Crewe instead of going by Ingleton.' Indeed, Midland passengers were often forced to walk between the two rival stations at Ingleton, though there were railway lines between those stations, extending over the viaduct spanning the gorge of the Greta.

Allport's letter reflects the anger and frustration felt by the Midland. It also shows why the company was determined to move its own traffic to Scotland on Midland metals. In 1865, when hundreds of square miles of the Pennines were without railways, a North of England Union Railway was proposed by Lord Wharncliffe, whose possessions included an estate in upper Wensleydale, and by other local gentlemen. They were confident enough to introduce a Bill to Parliament dealing with the construction of a railway between Settle and Hawes, with a branch from Horton to Clapham, a station on the 'Little' North-Western Railway. Hawes would be the junction of a branch to Sedbergh, and the main line would continue down Wensleydale to join up with systems in the east. It was a neat arrangement, making use of convenient dales.

The Bill was approved by the Commons, but before it could be considered by the Lords the Midland intervened, and it was agreed that the Bill should be withdrawn and reintroduced by the Midland in a modified form. The Midland, actively supported by two Scottish companies, the North British and the Glasgow and South Western Railway, would lay the tracks from Settle to Hawes but, more to the point, would continue a major line northwards, over the Pennines and up the Eden Valley, to Carlisle – the gateway to Scotland.

When the scheme for a Settle–Carlisle railway was made public in November, great excitement was generated at the towns and villages of the district. The new Bill was read before the Commons, and committed, early in 1866. In due course, it was approved. When the news reached Appleby, the church bells were rung. The Lords raised no objections, and Royal Assent was given on July 16. It was by no means the end of the matter. The Midland finances were not in good order, for it was already heavily committed to meeting the cost of extensions from Rowsley to Manchester, and from Bedford to St. Pancras, projects which were vital to its well-being. Now the share-holders were being asked to approve the raising of a further £2,200,000 for a line springing from inter-company rivalry: for self defence, indeed. Somewhat alarmed, the London and North-Western re-opened talks with the Midland, which led to a plan for a joint committee that would be responsible for working the Lancaster–Carlisle.

Meanwhile, the Midland had requested a period of seven years for the construction of the line. Parliament insisted that the work should be completed in five years. In September 1866, John Crossley directed the staking out of sections of the route, but it was done half-heartedly, against a background of talk of abandonment. Work came to a halt on the last day of the year, and the project lay idle for almost two years. When the Midland applied to Parliament for an Abandonment Bill, in 1869, Parliament – wary of such a practise – turned it down. In any case, the Settle–Carlisle was now enthusiastically supported by landowners who had previously opposed it, and the Scottish railway companies favoured it. So operations were resumed; the shareholders voted £550,000, and tenders were invited for four contracts (to cover the railway construction between Settle and Carlisle), plus another contract (for the branch line to Hawes). Engineers and workmen were in the Ribblehead area, the setting for some of the largest works, in the autumn of 1869. Construction was in hand early in the following year.

John Crossley, as engineer-in-chief, prepared the plans. He had delayed his retirement from the Midland to see the line through to completion and, indeed, he died in 1878, the year in which the Hawes branch was opened. The construction of the Settle–Carlisle is popularly thought of as a navvy operation, but it benefited from techniques and applicances that had been improved through many years of experience. Vertical steam engines (similar to those used for constructing sewers in the big cities) were taken to the heads of projected tunnel shafts. Concrete was used as the foundation for some viaducts. 'Steam travellers' operated on wooden framing, lifting stones of considerable size and weight into position on the piers. In 1873, a new Burleigh rock drill was being used at Birkett Tunnel, enabling a hole a foot deep to be made in five minutes.

The labour force was large, and peaked at about 6,000. Hundreds of horses hauled wagons on tramways from the new cuttings to where embankments were required. It was to be written that the line penetrated 'a region through which nothing but unlimited capital and indomitable energy could have carried it.' The workforce had to cope with a grim period of weather. Work was hampered by torrential rain, and by the torrents that rushed into the ends of incompleted tunnels. Snow and frost bound the fell country for months on end. A minor earthquake shook the huts standing on the wild face of Blea Moor.

The Pennine climate, characterised by a cold late spring, cloudy and moist summer, a settled autumn and a hard, long winter, was to test the resolution of those who operated the Settle–Carlisle line once the large navvy force had departed. The Helm Wind is a fearful draught brewed up about High Cup Nick, on the northern Pennines. A fireman at Carlisle observed that he once knew it to blow coal from his shovel as his train moved through the Eden Valley. Waterfalls, cascading down the steep slopes of Mallerstang Edge, are blown back on themselves, giving the effect of a smoking fellside. Snow fences at Dent are a mute testimony to the prevalence of winter snow. Periods of drought have not been unknown, and in recent times a DMU used by 'Dalesrail' ran low on water at Garsdale and had its water tank replenished by cheerful volunteers carrying buckets, and even a watering can. It is said that the cannister holding the signalman's drinking water was purloined!

The workforce – footplate staff, men at station and signal box, and those who maintain the permanent way – have not lacked loyalty and dedication. A Carlisle man, John Mayblin, drove the re-built Kirtley 2–4–0 which hauled the first passenger train in 1876. Midland locomotives were for a time lacking in power, and double-heading was not uncommon. Then came the celebrated compound engines and, in the inter-war years, the Claughtons and Jubilees, followed during the 1939–45 war by re-built Royal Scots. In the later days of steam, even the mighty Stanier worked the line. When the diesel age dawned, the prototype Deltic was tested on the Settle–Carlisle line, where many fine steam locomotives had been put through their paces.

When one of the authors travelled in the cab of a northward-bound Class 45, he saw the driver sitting in comfort, coaxing power from a unit with the capacity of 2,500 h.p. Our speed was limited to 60 m.p.h., but away to the west crack expresses on the electrified Lancaster–Carlisle were storming Shap at 100 miles an hour, with the drivers easing them off a little on reaching the top of that awesome bank.

The Midland always tended to regard the Settle–Carlisle as a means to an end, and even in its heyday there were no more than six through local trains daily, supplemented by Carlisle to Appleby locals and workings from Hellifield to Horton or Hawes Junction. On Sundays, there were no trains in the day at all. Another snoop was made at the London and North-Western by attempting to capture traffic to and from Penrith. The station at Langwathby, on the Settle–Carlisle, is only five miles from this northern gateway to the Lake District, and horse teams used to shuttle between the two points. Horse charabanc trips were run to the shores of Ullswater. On the Hawes branch, the North Eastern Railway worked five trains each way daily between Northallerton and Hawes Junction.

The Settle–Carlisle was thrashed almost to death during two world wars, when it was used for the conveyance of troops and vital war equipment. A number of bridges was strengthened to allow for the movement of the heaviest available locomotives, which dwarfed the Kirtleys originally employed on the line. After the 1939–45 war, to the end of the steam period, a bewildering – but fascinating – variety of locomotives appeared on the line.

A bright aspect of recent years was the introduction of the *Dalesrail* service, leading to the re-opening of a number of stations, and a passenger system, once a month, integrated to bus services, enabling users to penetrate deeply into the Dales country well within a day. It was an echo of the sort of enterprise shown by the Midland in its early period operating the Settle–Carlisle, and a forerunner of the more startling developments described in the chapter 'Run-down and Revival' (pages 70 - 82).

The current attempt by British Rail to close the line sprang from announcements of the sad condition of Ribblehead viaduct after standing for well over a century in one of the wettest parts of the North, and exposed to westerly gales. The cost of a new viaduct has been estimated in millions of pounds.

Mr John Watson, M.P. for Skipton Division, has summed up the feelings of many by observing: 'Apart from its economic significance, its strategic value and its environmental advantages, the Settle to Carlisle line reflects some of the most heroic achievements of Britain's railway age. Many men and women died to build the line and construct the (Ribblehead) viaduct. It properly occupies a position of immense importance in our history. Its closure would indeed be tragic . . .'

A Parliamentary Committee considers the Settle–Carlisle Bill.

The Terrain

A PHOTOGRAPH of the Northern Pennines taken from a satellite clearly shows the course of the Settle–Carlisle railway. From a height of 570 miles, the camera's eye is capable of registering several of the main features. It shows, with clarity, why the Midland was able to consider taking a central course to Scotland, between the lines of its rival companies.

The heads of two north–south valleys, Ribble and Eden, came within a few miles of each other. The intervening terrain would be difficult to span, but if immense viaducts were constructed to cross the deeper gills, and tunnels were made at Blea Moor and Rise Hill, the connection could have acceptable gradients, concluded the Midland surveyors. Many less dedicated people had pronounced the area uncrossable.

It was the watershed which ruled the Midland's thoughts. With a ruling gradient of 1 in 100, the Settle–Carlisle must begin to climb immediately at Settle Junction (in the south) and in the Appleby area (to the north) so that the 1,169 feet at Aisgill Moor would be cleared comfortably. Settle Junction is, indeed, much nearer Long Preston than was first intended. No one doubted that the most difficult stretch would be that between Blea Moor and Aisgill, 10 miles, through Camden's 'horrid silent wilderness.' It was a bleak area, indeed. The boundary of Mallerstang parish once included the instructions: ' ... thence to a hurrock of stones at the east end of Swarth Fell, called Swarth Fell Pike, thence to a hurrock of stones in Galloway Gates, thence as Heaven water deals to Blandston ...'

The railway used the hillsides, rather than the bottoms of the dales. It was laid on ledges cut from lonely fells; it leapt dramatically across the gills, and went underground where the fells obtruded or where the cuttings would have had to be of such a depth as to induce landslip during the railway's operational life. A writer in the *Carlisle Patriot* referred to the central part of the route taken by the Settle–Carlisle as 'a continued succession of high hills with intervening valleys, so that the line is alternately carried over viaducts, or through cuttings, or under hills hundreds of feet in height.'

The same glaciers that had conveniently gouged the tiny valleys into the only conceivable route for the line also deposited thousands of tons of boulder clay. Embankments refused to bind, whole hillsides slid bodily into the valleys and at Dandry Mire, for two years, the peat swallowed up all the tipped material which should have been rising as an embankment, so much so that the engineers had to plan a 10-arch viaduct instead.

Parliament granted the Midland a strip of land, and it was left to the company's valuers, through negotiation with the landowners, to acquire it. A young Tasmanian surveyor called Charles Stanley Sharland, a member of Crossley's staff, achieved fame when he walked from Carlisle to Settle in 10 days, taking surveys and levels. It was related that when he and his men reached Gearstones, near Ribblehead, they were trapped at the inn for a considerable period because of a heavy snowfall, and that Sharland tunnelled through a drift so that water could be taken from a trough in the yard. (Sharland did not live to see the railway completed; he died at Torquay at the age of 26).

William Crackanthorpe, of Newbiggin, encountered Midland surveyors at his favourite stand of oaks; he asked that the largest and finest tree might be spared, and the surveyors agreed. Why did he wish to preserve that tree? 'To hang you and all the engineers of the Midland Railway upon it, for daring to come here at all!'

In the early 1870s, the weather more than lived up to its reputation. At Dent Head during 1872 there were 92 inches of rain, compared with the average of 68 inches, and at Kirkby Stephen 60 inches fell, against an average of 37. Wet weather did not by itself delay the masons; they feared the high winds, to which they were exposed as they strode on the wooden frames which surrounded the emergent piers of the viaducts. Flooding was an ever-present risk in the stub-ends of the tunnels. For weeks in winter, work was held up because of snow and ice.

We have already mentioned the boulder clay. Disturb it in wet weather, and it takes on the consistency of Yorkshire pudding mixture, whereas in hot, dry conditions it hardened until it might bend a pickaxe. One despairing engineer told F. S. Williams: 'I have known the men blast the boulder clay like rock, and within a few hours have to ladle out the same stuff from the same spot like soup in buckets. Or a man strikes a blow with his pick at what he thinks is clay, but there is a great boulder underneath almost as hard as iron, and the man's wrists, arms and body are so shaken by the shock that, disgusted, he flings down his tools, asks for his money, and is off.' In *Wildman's Household Almanack* (1874) it was related: 'The "slurry" slips out of the embankments and sticks to the tip wagons, often causing these to come badly over the "tip head" and damaging it greatly; besides the expense of getting the wagon again on the embankment some 60 feet up.'

A Century
of Change

The beginning – and the end? Ribblehead viaduct under construction about 1873. Just over a century later, in 1981, the allegedly serious condition of this viaduct precipitated the most hotly-contested rail closure proposal ever seen in Britain. *(British Railways)*

Bridge building in progress. Above: Dent Head viaduct, clearly showing the immense amount of timbering which was required. Below: Crowdundle viaduct in the Eden Valley, with the arches turned but the embankment not yet reared against the strong terminal pier. *(British Railways)*

Midland glory, as epitomised by an up clerestory-roofed express passing through Hawes Junction in charge of a '2606-10' class 4-4-0. A North Eastern train from Hawes is in the background. *(per Rixon Bucknall)*

Midland pride was severely dented by the tragic Hawes Junction and Ais Gill accidents in 1910 and 1913. Here an up express cautiously passes the tarpaulin-sheeted wreckage of the latter disaster.

L.M.S. days. Compound No. 1045 on a six-coach express at Armathwaite. *(E. E. Smith)*

The slightly tarnished image of the early B.R. period. 2-6-2T No. 41206 leaves Settle with 'The Bonnyface' – the afternoon Hawes–Bradford stopping service. *(Derek Cross)*

Snow has frequently interrupted the regular flow of traffic on the Settle–Carlisle. Top: An engine barely protruding above the drifts at Ais Gill in 1946 when blizzards closed the line for two months. Bottom: The Edinburgh–London sleeping car express, marooned between Rise Hill and Dent in January 1963. *(Jack Sedgwick)*

The diesel age. Above: A stopping train leaves Settle during the period from 1966 when local services were operated by diesel units, prior to withdrawal in 1970. Below: Diesel-hauled special trains pass at Dent during the centenary celebrations on a rainswept May 1st, 1976. *(G. W. Morrison)*

Return of steam! 5MT No. 5305 breasts Ais Gill summit in magnificent style – and superb wintry weather conditions – with the up 'Cumbrian Mountain Express' in March 1980. *(Peter Fox)*

Revival! One of the pioneer Dales Rail trains disgorges its passengers at Appleby on a sunny summer's day in 1975. *(Yorkshire Dales National Park)*

The workers demonstrated that not only faith moves mountains; they set about making quite substantial changes to the local topography. Intake Embankment, above Mallerstang, claimed 260,000 cubic yards of material, being 400 yards long and 76 feet high in the centre. About 250,000 cubic yards of ballast formed the high embankment just north of Settle. Some 100,000 cubic yards of 'slurry' were removed to make a cutting near Horton-in-Ribblesdale. Bad weather, and sloppy boulder clay, 'have tended much to promote the roving habits of the men.' Yet the glacial clay had an important use at Ribblehead. The clay on Batty Moss was found to be free from limestone pebbles, and so it was used for brick-making, the bricks being needed for lining the arches of the viaduct and for reinforcing sections of Blea Moor tunnel.

Everyone who has responded to the savage appeal of the Settle–Carlisle knows the mountain stretch between the headwaters of Ribble and Eden. A traveller up the valley of the Ribble is never far from the line. It is a different matter in the Eden Valley, which is

vast, fanning out into a plain when it is close to the sea. The Settle–Carlisle loses itself in the vastness, between the Cumbrian Mountains and the unbroken barrier of the North Pennines. Smardale Viaduct is clearly seen from the Brough–Appleby road, but vanishes from sight at closer range, and the visitor uses a network of little roads near Crosby Garrett to approach it.

Many of the problems in Edenvale were connected with the river, for although surveyors charted a course on higher ground – thinking all the time of the crossing at the watershed – the Settle–Carlisle must inevitably cross the river. This it did for the first time at Ormside, where an imposing viaduct was constructed.

Curiously, the nearer Carlisle is approached, and the wilder becomes the scenery, until it is like a tract from the Scottish Highlands. We refer to the area of the Eden Gorge, with its heather and pinewoods. Three tunnels, and three viaducts, were needed, and making them was not especially difficult. It was the earthmoving at Edenbrows that frustrated the builders. Between Armathwaite and High Stand Gill, the railway occupies the customary hillside ledge. In the 1870s a landslip developed. Five acres of ground were affected. The engineers needed all their wits to overcome this awesome setback.

Viaducts and Tunnels

THE VIADUCTS of the Settle–Carlisle make the greatest visual appeal; none is more prominent than Ribblehead, the piers of which are set deeply in Batty Moss, under the gaze of Whernside and at the approach to that railway-builder's nightmare, Blea Moor. Having 24 arches, and a length of 1,328 feet, Ribblehead viaduct is buttressed by immense embankments. The stone for the viaduct – all limestone – came mainly from Littledale and, indeed, the viaduct was constructed from north to south.

So great was this structure to be that work on it began immediately. Trial borings were made during the first winter, 1869–70. Shafts were sunk to the solid rock, 25 feet down through peat and clay. A story began to circulate that in this peaty area, the piers were being supported by bales of wool. The reality was that concrete was used, and up to six feet in depth. (When, not many years later, a railway was constructed between Fort William and Mallaig, in north-west Scotland, viaducts were being made entirely of concrete).

During the construction of the viaduct, there would seem to be as much timber as stone. The piers emerging from the shafts were enmeshed by a light timber stage, on which could run a mobile crane, a 'steam traveller.' When the height of the masonry reached that of the gantry, fresh timbers were added. The work was carefully programmed so that it was unnecessary to simultaneously timber throughout the viaduct's length. When the arches of one section had been turned, the heavy baulks were simply moved to where more piers were emerging from the moor.

Much thought went into the selection of the stone, and in due course a stream in Littledale was diverted to expose the finest beds of rock, which were robbed of over 30,000 cubic yards of material. (The stream, a continual threat to the Settle–Carlisle, was eventually made to flow in a stone trough which was lined with hot asphalt). From Littledale, the stone was borne by tramway and, dressed, the grey limestone was lifted into position. An engine was used for mixing the mortar.

Notice, at Ribblehead, that every sixth pier is thicker than the others, so that if one pier fell it would take only five other piers with

An impression of Ribblehead Viaduct and 'Bog Cart'.

it. Many of the masons were Welsh, and in March 1872 they were on strike for a week for better wages. The outcome is not known, but before they were 'out' the pay was 6s. 3d. for a nine hour day, 6s. 11d. for 10 hours in summer. About 100 men were at work on the viaduct at any given time; the arches were lined with bricks made locally.

The engineers were proud of their efforts. The 45 feet spans were assembled on wooden framing, and when each frame was removed the arch (it was claimed) dropped a mere quarter of an inch. The arches were then covered with concrete, and in turn overlaid with asphalt to deflect rainwater from the brickwork.

Dent Head, north of Blea Moor, has 10 spans, a length of 596 feet and a maximum height of 100 feet – or more than that at Ribblehead. The timber staging for Dent Head was erected by midsummer, 1873, and by December six of the 10 arches were ready for turning; only one pier had yet to be started. A 'blue' variety of limestone, quarried locally, was used for the work.

Arten Gill, another major water-carved valley in the side of the valley of the Dee, is spanned by a viaduct which looks impossibly slender, and yet has immense strength, having a length of 660 feet, 11 spans, and a maximum height of 117 feet. Excavations to find a firm footing for some of the piers extended to a depth of over 50 feet in the sides of the gills. The stone used was of local origin: dark, highly fossilised, known as 'Dent marble'. The arches were turned with stone, not brick.

Each pier on Arten Gill is 15 feet thick at the bottom, gradually tapering to six and a half feet at the top. Dressed stone was transported to the staging in tramway bogies, and a 'steam traveller' lifted the blocks and deposited them exactly where they were needed. Because sand was unobtainable locally, the mortar was made of lime and burnt clay, being referred to as 'Crossley Cement'.

One viaduct was built in desperation. Dandry Mire makes a 12-span crossing of what used to be a notorious moss. The plan was to create an embankment, but Dandry Mire had an insatiable appetite for tipped material. Every tip wagon taken to the area had to be conveyed by road from Sedbergh, and the carriage on each was a guinea. A hundred wagons were in regular use, and tipping went on for two years. The continuous wet weather, and the sogginess of the mire, merely caused the peat to rise up on either side. Banks 12 feet wide or more in height appeared, one bank extending 24 yards beyond the Midland's boundary. Frustrated engineers decided that Dandry Mire should have a viaduct. At the time the decision was taken in 1872, the nearby Moorcock viaduct was complete apart from the coping stones.

Smardale viaduct, in the Eden Valley, carries the line over the Scandal Beck in 12 lofty arches to a height of 130 feet. Some of the trial boreholes probed for 20 feet to the underlying rock, and in due course some 60,000 tons of limestone were brought in. Smardale none the less looks dainty when seen from a distance. The original design included a second set of six arches at a lower level between two heavy piers, but the engineers confidentally dispensed with the idea.

Smardale Viaduct, in the Eden Valley.

There were early difficulties at Ormside viaduct, for one of the piers had to stand in the river. The engineers made a miniature coffer dam of inch board. A similar dam, employed at Eden Lacy, near Little Salkeld, was destroyed by a river in spate in 1872. Long Marton viaduct looks especially smart, for red and white stones were used. The most ingenious viaduct is seen by few people. It spans the Ribble in the gorge near Stainforth, and though of large size was set on the skew and fashioned so as to allow for the all-important gradient of 1 in 100 - considerations that must have created some headaches among the designers and masons.

There are many bridges of modest size but great interest, including an iron girder bridge between Langcliffe and the mills. Many of the workforce, wearing clogs, trudged down a lane, across the bridge, and along the continuation of the lane, and in winter they were grateful for the light from gas lamps to brighten the final stretch of the journey.

The Tunnels

VIEW BLEA MOOR from afar, and you see the old tramways winding between heaps of rock blasted at the heart of the hill and raised up the shafts by steam-winch during over four years of tunnelling. Blea Moor tunnel, of 2,629 yards, is the most famous on the Settle–Carlisle. The ventilation shafts break the moorland surface as circular structures of brick, like red pimples on the hill's rugged pate. Fine mesh prevents 'foreign bodies' from descending to the railway tracks hundreds of feet below. Years ago, one of us joined an inspection party in Blea Moor tunnel, viewing the shafts from below. These brick-lined tubes, 10 feet in diameter, gleamed with moisture. Garlands had been placed at intervals to catch water and lead it into fallpipes from which it flows into the main drains.

The tunnelling project, as severe as any task on the line, cost £45 a yard, and relays of men endured gloomy, wet conditions. Tramways were needed to take material to the hilltop, where the shafts would be driven, and the first of these was laid by men working from Dent Head, to the north. Soon an 'iron road' was laid for two and a half miles from Batty Moss. Light engines and trucks ran on tramways with moderate gradients, and a tramway on steeper ground was operated by a wire rope connected to a fixed engine. Another tramway was self-acting, the weight of trucks bearing millstone grit from a local quarry being more than sufficient to draw up strings of empty trucks.

Seven stationary engines were needed on and around Blea Moor, two of them winding up materials on either side of the hill, the other being placed at the heads of the shafts, to draw up debris from workings far below, and to lower supplies of bricks and mortar needed for lining the tunnel. 'An engine was also used to lower or raise the commuting workers. Appliances were needed to pump water from the completed sections, and to supply air to the workers. The fuel for all this machinery was coal, conveyed up the Moor first by donkeys and then in trollies, where the coal was often 'crowned with bags of flour and other domestic commodities' for the workers and their families, who were accommodated in huts.

Miners, the folk-heroes of Blea Moor, worked by candlelight, and the bill for tallow candles was £50 a month. Holes for the explosives were drilled by hand, and dynamite, then a novelly, was packed into the holes and ignited by means of a time fuse. The bill for dynamite was £200 a ton, a major part of the cost being its transportation by road from Newcastle to Carlisle. The railways would not take the risk of handling it. The debris from the headings was cleared away by labourers. If the heading was far into the hill, the rock was conveyed up a shaft in a 'skep', but material displaced at an end of the tunnel was removed by horse-drawn trolley. The tunnel horses were well groomed, bedecked with ribbons by their proud drivers.

Some 300 miners, bricklayers and labourers worked in Blea Moor tunnel at the peak of the activity. Less than a dozen serious accidents are known. Since the line was opened, there has been a regular inspection of the tunnel's crown, haunches and sidewalls. Tablets on the walls note the distance from the tunnel mouth at the southern end, so any part of the masonry can have its position noted exactly. Blea Moor holds the rusted remains of a gong installed as a warning device when an outer distant signal was placed in the tunnel following the installation of loop lines at Blea Moor. The gong warned the footplate men to look for the signal, but it never worked properly and was removed. A signal was placed outside the tunnel.

The other major obstruction to the railway-builders on the mountain stretch was Rise Hill, north of Dent Station. At 1,213 yards in length, it was a baby when compared with Blea Moor, but it inherited some of the awkward traits of its parents. Rise Hill was remote from roads and villages, and so accommodation for hundreds of men was provided by the contractors. Men used a tramway that was three-quarters of a mile long; they sat in bogies and were hauled up from Garsdale by steam engine. The tramway also carried coal, railway material and provisions.

At Rise Hill, the excavated hillside material – little more than slush in places – adhered to the tools like treacle and was removed chiefly by grafting tools and water buckets. Care was taken when rock was blasted, but pieces weighing 15 cwt. were known to fly a distance of 20 yards. A visitor noticed the 'dimly burning candles, uncouth-looking wagons standing on the rails or moving to and fro, men at the facings, some above and some below, with their

numerous lights like twinkling stars in a hazy night, the noise of the twirling drills beneath the terrible force of big hammers wielded by stalwart men, the *hac-hac* or half-sepulchral groan at each stroke, the murky vapour, the chilling damp and the thick breathing.' Rise Hill has two air shafts, the deepest being of 147 feet.

The Settle–Carlisle leaves Mallerstang when it enters the 424-yard long Birkett tunnel, which lies exactly on the Great Pennine Fault. In its making, shale, magnesium limestone, mountain limestone, grit, slate, iron, coal and a workable vein of lead were all discovered. There was an alarming rock fall. On being shown this geological hotch-potch, John Crossley remarked that it was the most curious combination he had ever seen. Helm tunnel, near Ormside, is 600 yards long. When it was completed in 1873, the entire space was brilliantly illuminated as a company of engineers and local people assembled, in the Victorian way, for mutual congratulation.

Culgaith tunnel, 661 yards long, was driven through hard red marl; there is but one ventilation shaft. The line emerges into daylight only yards from the river Eden, and the two are never more than a mile apart until beyond Cotehill. The railway is in the open for only a quarter of a mile before it vanishes into Waste Bank tunnel, which is extremely short – a case where a cutting might have been adequate, but the engineers shrewdly decided to leave it roofed in case of landslip. Like all the tunnels north of this point, it was cut through red sandstone.

Among the features of the Settle–Carlisle which would be counted as minor compared with the main tunnels, but are immense in their own roles, are some culverts. The Keld Beck culvert assists a flow of water into the upper Dee. The ground hereabouts has an awesome slope, and so the culvert was made in steps. Cow Gill is crossed by an embankment about 100 feet high, and its culvert, shaped like a Gothic arch, is an impressive 540 feet in length.

The Stations

NINETEEN stations were constructed along the 72 miles of the Settle–Carlisle. The 20th station appeared at Hawes, in Wensleydale. The Midland, despite its cash problems, built substantially and with style, its buildings being faced with stone, and the roofs steeply-pitched, as though to allow for the worst excesses of the Pennine climate. At Settle, much freestone was used, and further up the dale there is grey limestone. Across the 'tops', in the Eden Valley, the Midland made use of local sandstone, so that each station has a rosy hue in sunshine.

The basic design of a country station was of twin pavilions, separated by a glazed front porch.

Settle: The Victorian flavour was apparent until recent times. In the Stationmaster's office in winter, the hissing gas jets, the high office furniture, and the steam trains thundering by in the darkness, seemed like elements in a mystery thriller. In 1976, when the centenary of the line was celebrated, a marquee was erected in the station yard, with a canvas corridor leading to the station buildings, through which passengers on a special centenary train alighted for a banquet. The carriages of which the special train was composed included some ancient stock from the National Railway Museum; seen after dark, by artificial light, they evoked the drama of Victorian times.

Settle station, complete with goods yard and shed, was built in 'Gothic' style of Bradford stone. Vast quantities of material were tipped to create the station yard, and it was here that one of the big clearance sales took place on the line's completion. The sidings have been lifted and the goods-shed demolished but the tank house endures. The stationmaster's house is privately owned.

Always a busy station, Settle benefited from a caring staff and regularly won prizes for its garden and the cleanliness of its buildings.

Horton-in-Ribblesdale: The hillside nature of the Settle–Carlisle is evident here, for the station has a steep approach road and appears to stand on a ledge. Stationmaster Jim Taylor had oversight of the goods traffic emanating from the nearby Beecroft Quarry – an evening train was called 'Limey' – and yet he managed to create a fine station garden and also hold exhibitions of art in the waiting room.

Ribblehead: A long approach road was made from the turnpike road to the station, and for years the private road was used for autumnal sheep sales, the station itself providing a handy point of embarkation for stock bought by outside dealers. Religious services were held in the waiting room from springtime, 1880, and they had the benign approval of the Midland. The vicar of Ingleton conducted the services, and there was for many years a harmonium in the waiting room.

Much later, Ribblehead became a weather station, the stationmaster having the additional responsibility of taking note of the weather and forwarding the details at hourly intervals to the Air Ministry, Ribblehead being considered important as one of the few highland stations in the North. A wind velocity of 50 knots was reasonably common (on some days it reached 70 knots, with gales from the west battering the nearby viaduct to the extent of ripping tarpaulin covers from goods wagons of passing trains). In January, 1954, a gale stopped three trains. The rain gauge at Ribblehead recorded 109½ inches of rain in 1954, the average rainfall being about 70 inches.

Dent: When the Settle–Carlisle was opened for a regular passenger train service in May, 1876, Dent station had not been finished. There were differences of opinion about where it should be placed. Some people preferred a site to the south, in which case the station would have been called Dent Head. Dent station, viewed from the valley road, looks improbable, being perched high on the fell, served by a winding road that climbs 450 feet in little more than half a mile, the gradient of the road being 1 in 5. Coal traffic was important in the early days (most Dales families had hitherto burnt peat), and, though steep, the road favoured the laden, horse-drawn wagons, which were usually empty when making the ascent.

Dent station, at an elevation of 1,100 feet, has the highest platforms of any English mainline rail system. The stationmaster's house, now privately owned, stands slightly higher than the station and was provided – in Midland days – with double-glazing. At Dent station, dilapidated snow fences, made of upreared sleepers, accentuate the feeling of remoteness. A billet was provided for men on special snow-clearing duty, and in 1963 food was sent up to them from the railway refreshment room at Preston. A special force of 500 men, including soldiers and German prisoners-of-war, was mustered to cope with the drifts of 1947. During the 1963 snowfall, cornices reared elegantly but dangerously over 20 foot drifts at the edge of the cutting; snow was loaded into wagons and tipped over Dent Head viaduct. No regular trains passed through Dent station for five days, and passengers in a marooned sleeping car train had to be heroically rescued.

The buildings were used as a Dales centre by boys from a Lancashire school. A cache of old material in the roof included counterfoils for first-class rail tickets in 1883, when you could travel from Dent to Hawes for 1s.11d; to Blackburn for 7s.2d; to Northallerton for 5s.11d and to Liverpool for 12s.1d. Housemartins under the eaves at Dent station are among the highest-nesting birds of this species in the country.

Garsdale: Two miles from the north portal of Rise Hill Tunnel is Garsdale station, which at other stages of its existence was called Hawes Junction, Hawes Junction and Garsdale, and Garsdale for Hawes. It is over three miles from any sizeable community, but nevertheless is the only true junction station on the Settle–Carlisle. The company had hoped to establish here an engine shed for two dozen locomotives, and 30 cottages were to be constructed for their employees. The shed scheme was abandoned when finances were cramped during the closing stages of building the line, but in the halcyon days before the 1914–18 war the station saw plenty of locomotive activity. Almost every train was double-headed and the pilots were detached here to be turned before returning as light engines to Hellifield or Carlisle. It was nothing unusual for the signalman to have over half a dozen light engines to handle.

With the decline and eventual end of piloting, the turntable became obsolete and was removed several years before the end of steam haulage. It is a pity, for it was one of the most interesting features of the line and also the scene of a most improbable yet true happening. One wild night an engine was being turned when it was caught broadside on by a severe wind and went on spinning like a merry-go-round for some minutes. Eventually the staff hit on the idea of pouring sand into the well of the turntable and only in this way was the locomotive-turned-into-a-roundabout brought to a standstill. To prevent any possible repetition the turntable was surrounded by a stockade, made of old sleepers.

Garsdale did eventually get a very small engine shed, used not by the Midland but by the North-Eastern Railway, which usually worked the service to Hawes. It was burned down in 1917, rebuilt and finally closed in 1939.

The folk at Garsdale station formed their own distinctive little community, especially before 1959. It was in that year that the Wensleydale line was closed to passenger traffic. If a ghostly train were to be seen on moonlit nights, it would surely be the ghost of

Bonnyface, the Hawes–Bradford train, which was put on Garsdale's famous stockaded turntable and travelled tender first to Hawes, returning at 4.25 p.m. The name 'Bonnyface' is intriguing. Some people say the train was named after a particularly ugly permanent way inspector. It is also related that when their day's work was almost over, the locomotive's face was the bonniest they saw during their shift.

The Tank House, demolished in 1971, held a receptacle for 80,000 gallons of water. From the 1930s, until the coming of television caused interest in rural events to dwindle, Garsdalians used the Tank House as a centre for domino and whist drives, potato pie suppers and concerts. A thoughtful lady passenger donated to Garsdale a 200-volume library. At the Tank House, the 'wallflowers' at dances sat on red-upholstered seats that were taken from a scrapped railway carriage. The buffet was a wheel-less railway carriage of Midland ancestry, and it sported its original doors. Some of the events held at the Tank House raised up to £40 for the Bradford Royal Infirmary. When Mr Douglas Cobb was the stationmaster in 1953, he started a platform garden, importing the soil, and cheerfully considering growing flowers on a windswept platform over 1,000 feet above sea level.

No. 13 Railway Cottages at Garsdale bore the grand name Temperance Hotel. Here lived Mr and Mrs Reuben Alton, who provided accommodation, mainly for commercial travellers. In 1947, the main line was snowblocked for weeks, but trains continued to run from Hawes to Garsdale, and food for the populace was stacked on the engine. That was the time when the worth of the railway in serving a rural population was amply demonstrated, though snowploughs used on the roads were decked with fodder for the stock, and the R.A.F. delivered bales of hay by air. One pilot was so exact in his haydrop that a bale went through a farmhouse roof.

Kirkby Stephen West: The longest run between two stations on the Settle–Carlisle used to be the 9¾ miles between Garsdale and Kirkby Stephen. (In 1884, a station was proposed for Mallerstang, and the Midland agreed to provide it if the residents of the dale would build a road at a cost of £2,200. Lord Hothfield offered the land for the site, but the necessary money could not be found). Kirkby Stephen West station is, like so many others on this railway, a considerable distance from the place it purported to serve. The distance from here to the centre of the town is 1½ miles. It was once named Kirkby Stephen and Ravenstonedale, although the village which inspired such a lengthy title is 3½ miles distant.

Eden Valley: Crosby Garrett station was built in a cutting 55 feet deep. Appleby has some impressively-long platforms, one of them extending to 200 yards. The station stands at the highest point of the town, and at 525 feet the engineers had to look hard and long for a dependable water supply for the locomotives, which needed 50,000 gallons a day. The nearest hill streams were three miles away. So a pumping engine was established at the side of the Eden, and water was raised 140 feet to a tank at the station. Culgaith station is, architecturally, in a different style from any of the others on the Settle–Carlisle. Here is the first level crossing; it lies alongside the end of the platform. Langwathby station was originally known as Longwathby. Little Salkeld is immediately preceded by the seven spans of Little Salkeld or Dodd's Mill Viaduct. At Lazonby, a cutting was intended but the railway was so close to the Rectory the Midland was prevailed upon to excavate a tunnel so that the cleric would not be disturbed by passing trains. Armathwaite, in the broad valley, lies close to the Eden Gorge, of which Williams wrote: 'The scenery at this point is such that the traveller will often wish he were able to stop the train every few minutes to enjoy it.' Since its closure in 1952, Cotehill station, originally Knott Hill, has virtually ceased to exist.

Carlisle: The Citadel Station – built of Yorkshire stone – in a style which has been termed 'Victorian Tudor' – was opened in 1847. In pre-grouping days, Midland trains were just one of a crowd, and a very inferior member at that, for this was no less than the seventh company to use the joint station. Imposing neo-Tudor fireplaces adorn the refreshment room, and the stationmaster's office has the crests of the original private companies, along with those of L.M.S. and BR. In the 1960s, Carlisle Citidal closed for the first time in its history; it was shut for part of Christmas Day.

Eden Gorge and diminutive train.

On The Rails

MATTHEW KIRTLEY became locomotive superintendent of the Midland Railway in 1841, at the age of 28. He did not live to see the completion of the Settle–Carlisle, for he died in 1873 after being in office for 32 years. Yet it was a Kirtley locomotive that hauled the first passenger express over the line, and Kirtleys served it well in the early years. They had a 2–4–0 wheel arrangement, and their spartan cabs offered the drivers little protection from the fury of Pennine weather. Their proud drivers said that they could do anything but talk; they rejoiced in the fact that 'the harder they were thumped, the better they liked it.'

Midland Railway locomotives went through three changes of livery in a short space of time. At the date of opening, the colour was dark green throughout, but in the following year it was changed to blue-green, with a black edge and white lining. 'Midland red' was adopted in 1883, the pick-out lines being black edged with yellow.

Kirtley was succeeded by Samuel Johnson, and he presided over locomotive development during a period which saw a change to compounding on the Settle–Carlisle. Trains were becoming heavier; the small locomotives had frequently to be used in pairs. Johnson's flair in introducing 4–4–0s increased power without substantially increasing operating costs. He produced some of the most beautiful locomotives ever seen. The 4–4–0s, in various guises, handled the bulk of the traffic right through to the 1930s, being built by Johnson, his successor Richard Deeley and, after the grouping, by the London, Midland and Scottish Railway. By the late 1920s, trains were becoming too heavy even for the Compounds. They, in turn, climbed down the ladder to be used on pilot and light duties. To the shame of many older drivers, they were ousted from the role of principal passenger locomotive on the Settle–Carlisle by the ex-London and North-Western Railway 'Claughtons'.

Under Sir William Stanier, who was locomotive superintendent of the L.M.S. railway, motive power on the line underwent many changes in the 1930s. The 'Patriots', the 'Jubilees' and the 'Class 5s', all of the 4–6–0 wheel arrangement, were introduced within a number of years; the 'Claughtons' were no longer seen. The outbreak of the 1939–45 war led to trains becoming even longer and heavier. Piloting having become an almost unprovidable luxury, the cry was for more powerful locomotives of increased weight. It was necessary for bridges to be strengthened to take locomotives of increased weight. Two 'Jubilees', which had been rebuilt with larger boilers, appeared in 1942. In the following year, rebuilt 'Scots', again of the 4–6–0 wheel arrangement, worked over the line for the first time, and they were capable of handling almost any train unaided. Six of them were eventually stationed at Holbeck; they handled almost all the expresses until 1960, when steam passenger working on the Settle–Carlisle reached its greatest variety as it stood on the brink of dissolution.

In 1961, some of the huge A3 Pacifics which had been constructed by Sir Nigel Gresley for the London and North Eastern Railway began operating from Holbeck. Locomotives which had evolved for working on the relatively easy East Coast route none the less put up some fine performances, and two years later they were sometimes supplemented by Class A1 Pacifics and the streamline A4s. The student of railway performance was elated by traffic on the Settle–Carlisle in its Indian summer, for the aforementioned locomotives were in the company of 'Class 5s', 'Jubilees' and 'Scots', as well as British Railways 4–6–2 'Britannias' and 'Clans'. In 1963, Type 4 diesels took charge of almost all the expresses. The locals, after being worked by a surprising variety of motive power, gave way, in April, 1966, to two-car diesel multiple units.

As far as freight working was concerned, from the date of opening until the late 1920s all traffic with but one exceptioon was handled by a single type of locomotive, the 0–6–0, which was turned out by the hundred by both the Midland and L.M.S. railways. The exception was some 2–6–0s introduced in 1889 during a time of acute locomotive shortage; these were American in origin, and conspicuously American in styling. Some of the 0–6–0s could travel quite fast. Ahrons observed: 'The Carlisle goods drivers were noted for high speed at which they worked their trains. The signalmen between Carlisle and Leeds would always give the Carlisle goods drivers "the road" even when they were within measurable distance of the following express passenger train, because the signalman knew that the goods train would keep clear, but when the Leeds goods drivers came along they were promptly shunted into the nearest siding until the passenger train had passed.'

After the grouping, some ex-Glasgow and South Western Railway 2–6–0s were tried over the line. These were followed by Sir Henry Fowler's Class 5F 2–6–0s. In the late 1930s, Stanier's mixed-traffic Class 5 4–6–0s and Class 8F 2–8–0s were introduced, and these – together with British Railways Standard 9F 2–10–0 – formed the mainstay of freight working until the end of steam operation.

The fact that the Settle–Carlisle is the most spectacular main line in Britain has always meant that it has been a venue for trials and experiments. The first tests were way back in 1886 when a new type of sanding gear was tried out. The results led Midland to adopt steam instead of compressed air for sanding purposes. After the grouping, engines of three of the old companies were tried against each other – a London and North Western 'Prince of Wales' 4–6–0, a Caledonian 2-cylinder simple 4–4–0 and a Midland Compound. The solid worth of the Compound, both in performance and economy, was confirmed. The L.M.S. went on to construct more of them.

Following nationalisation, a whole series of locomotives, ranging from an ex-Southern Railway 'Merchant Navy' to the then new British Railways standard types, were extensively tested on the route. Two locomotives, *John Milton*, a British Railways 'Britannia' Class, and *Duchess of Gloucester*, one of Sir William Stanier's 4–6–2 Pacifics, were loaded up to the equivalent of 900 tons, and two firemen took turns in producing sufficient steam to keep these colossal loads moving at 30 miles an hour.

The Long Drag itself has always been favoured for such trials, having a continuous gradient. The journey from Carlisle to Ais Gill is not all climbing; the line falls on no less than eight occasions and for this reason the working of southbound trains is always an easier task than those in the opposite direction – though as already related many a perspiring fireman was wearied by the time he saw the signal at Ais Gill after the very long 'drag' from the Eden Valley.

Of the diesel stock, the Class 45 has been the mainstay for many years, though with its eight-wheel bogey a problem was access to Glasgow Central Station. The Class 47, which first appeared in numbers on diverted expresses, and has a six-wheel bogey, became standard haulage for passengers going to Glasgow, the Class 45 being retained for use on freight trains.

Passenger Traffic

IT WAS ANNOUNCED in 1876: 'When opened for passenger traffic, the celebrated Pullman Cars will be run from London to Scotland, and vice versa, so that at night passengers will be able to retire to rest at one terminus and alight refreshed at the other in the morning.' Four years earlier, Allport had gone to America to meet George Pullman, whose name was to become inseparably linked with luxury travel. Allport was convinced that by introducing Pullman cars on the Midland, the company would find itself far ahead of its rivals. The first Pullmans arrived in England in 1874, From the opening of the Settle–Carlisle, they helped to give the new route distinction, being introduced on the day and night expresses from St. Pancras to Glasgow and Edinburgh.

Passengers who were travelling over the heights of Ais Gill on a chilling winter night were undoubtedly grateful to Allport, for at that time standard carriages on British railways systems were spartan in the extreme. They had no heating apart from flat foot-warmers obtainable at stations. These were always either too hot or stone cold. Pullman's inventive mind had produced the idea for a closed circuit of hot water pipes which operated from a boiler fired by an attendant, and they were lit by kerosene instead of the conventional rape-oil pot lamps. They were also richly decorated. The Pullmans were taken from the Settle–Carlisle after a short period. Though undoubtedly comfortable, they were excessively draughty, and the lack of compartments did not appeal to Victorian conservatism.

Allport was not so pre-occupied by the Pullman car that he ignored other types of carriages. Indeed, he carried through a revolution in the Midland's rolling stock, abolishing second class, upgrading the third class, and disposing of wooden seats in favour of seats that were upholstered. His actions, which brought a howl of protest from other railway companies, particularly the rival London and North-Western, were described as 'a Jacobinical blow at the sanctity of caste' and a very bad business step. He was also accused of 'pampering the working classes.' His move was undoubtedly the right one, and until well into this century, travellers to Scotland who went over Ais Gill had a far more comfortable journey than their fellow passengers going by way of Shap or the East Coast route. Allport must have been a satisfied man when he retired in 1880. He was presented with a cheque for £10,000 by the Midland Railway shareholders, and four years later he was knighted 'for services to the poor traveller.'

In 1876, there was basically a one day express from St. Pancras to Scotland, and this express was divided at Skipton into Glasgow and Edinburgh portions. Here, additional coaches from Leeds, Bradford, Manchester and Liverpool were also added. Later the carriages from Lancashire were attached at Hellifield. There was a corresponding service in the reverse direction as well as a night service. Semi-fasts between Leeds and Bradford and Scotland completed the picture.

North of Carlisle, the Midland trains ran over the metals of either the Glasgow and South Western Railway or the North British Railway, and these companies were decidedly unhappy about the amounts they had to pay out in carriage hire. They were pacified in 1879 when the tri-owned Midland Scottish Joint Stock came into operation. These were superb vehicles. The first class compartments were lined with dark blue broadcloth and panelled in mahogany with a sycamore veneer and an edging of bird's eye maple. French merino curtains drew across the windows and the elbows and door-panel squabs were trimmed with morocco leather.

Features of
the Line

The start of the 'Long Drag'. Settle Junction in 1961, with the Morecambe line diverging on the right. The buildings of the short-lived Junction station can just be seen behind the 'Blue Train' coaches en route from Bradford to Glasgow. *(Derek Cross)*

A reminder of better times, when the station gardens at Settle regularly won awards. In the picture is Stationmaster J. M. Taylor. *(Border Press Agency)*

One of the lesser features of the route is this attractive crossing of the Ribble at Helwith Bridge. 40094 heads north past the lowering bulk of Penyghent. *(G. W. Morrison)*

Ribblehead station – where only the up platform now survives. Above: 2-6-4T No. 42051 pauses on a down stopping train. *(Eric Treacy)* Below: Stationmaster Clark, who combined his railway duties with those of weather reporter for the Air Ministry, about to release a hydrogen balloon in order to determine the height of cloud layers. *(Geoffrey N. Wright)*

The majesty of Ribblehead viaduct as seen (above) in the low autumn sunshine of October 1981. 'Sir Nigel Gresley' is crossing with the Cumbrian Mountain Pullman. *(G. W. Morrison)* The early commercial postcard (below) shows the view of the viaduct from the Ribblehead station approach.

The lonely outpost of Blea Moor. Above: Rush hour in April 1967 with one freight already occupying the down loop and a Long Meg–Widnes anhydrite train just pulling into the up loop – both are hauled by 9F 2-10-0s. *(Derek Cross)* Below: The architecture of Blea Moor, showing the now ruined water tower and the railway cottages.

Viaducts in Dentdale. Above: Dent Head – note how the landscape is being changed by what many criticise as serried ranks of conifers. Below: The 117ft high arches of Arten Gill are crossed by 'Duchess of Hamilton' on a 13-coach Cumbrian Mountain Express. (*G. W. Morrison*)

Changes at Dent. Top: The primly-kept station in 1905. (*Locomotive & General Railway Photographs*) Bottom: The sad scene in 1981, with signal-box closed, signal arms removed, track lifting in progress and snow fences in ruin. (*G. W. Morrison*)

The black holes of the Settle–Carlisle. Top: The south portal of Rise Hill tunnel as seen from the footplate of a 9F 2-10-0. *(Derek Cross)*   Bottom: A tunnel ventilation shaft – this one is on Blea Moor.

Unique features of the line. Above: The water troughs at Garsdale which were the highest in the world – at one time they were steam-heated against frost. *(Geoffrey G. Hoare)* Below: The turntable at Garsdale was the only one in Britain to be surrounded by a stockade – as a protection against the wind. *(J. W. Armstrong)*

A double-headed freight crosses Dandry Mire viaduct, built after all efforts to make an embankment at this point had failed. *(G. W. Morrison)* **Below: Distinctive Midland architecture at Garsdale – the left-hand side of the building boasts both a drinking fountain and a post box.**

Ais Gill, where things ain't what they used to be. Top: The lay-out as viewed in the 1950s; the refuge sidings were once extensively used for detaching pilot engines which had assisted trains to the summit from either Hellifield or Carlisle. *(British Railways)*   Bottom: A 1981 study, following closure of the signal-box and removal of the sidings. *(G. W. Morrison)*

Sidelights at Ais Gill. Above: Inside the signal-box, with Wild Boar Fell visible in the background.   Below: The summit signboard of England's highest main-line railway.

Kirkby Stephen station in pristine splendour in 1905. Note especially the lamps and advertisements. *(Locomotive & General Railway Photographs)*

Smardale viaduct, between Kirkby Stephen and Crosby Garrett, was at 130 feet the highest on the Midland Railway. Passing under one of the arches was the North Eastern line from Darlington to Tebay.

Profile of Crosby Garrett, a station closed in 1952. The two upper photographs are taken from virtually the same point, with the engine of the goods train (opposite top) passing the former cattle dock and about to come alongside the remains of the platform. *(Derek Cross)* The bottom picture on this page well captures the flavour and spaciousness of the English country station, with the amply-proportioned stationmaster's house on the right. Staffing was also at a generous level, as shown by the group posed outside the signal-box in the lower photograph opposite.

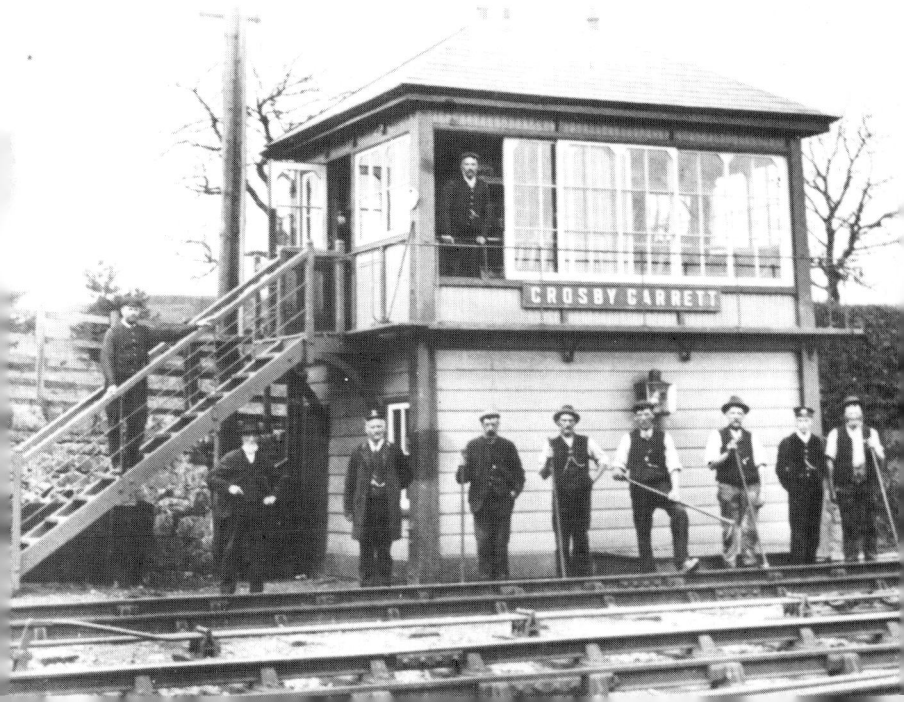

CROSBY GARRETT

Appleby, looking south in May 1967. This important intermediate station once handled a brisk trade in dairy products. *(Derek Cross)*

The attractive stretch of line in the Eden gorge between Lazonby and Cotehill. 45024 is emerging from one of the two tunnels at Baron Wood with the afternoon Glasgow–Nottingham express in April 1980. *(G. W. Morrison)*

Such luxury must have done much to mitigate the effects of the Pennine weather which would be so often rattling against the windows when the clouds were down.

Dining cars were not introduced until 1892 but cold luncheon baskets could be bought for three shillings at such points as Hellifield. They contained half a chicken with ham or tongue, hot or cold meats, salad, cheese, butter, and a half bottle of burgundy, claret, stout, apollinaris or a bottle of aerated water.

It was in the Edwardian years just before the 1914–18 war that passenger traffic over the Settle–Carlisle reached its zenith. There were three day expresses from St. Pancras, all of which carried through carriages for both Glasgow and Edinburgh. The 11.00 a.m. from London also conveyed a portion from Bristol, while the 1.30 p.m. departure ran in separate portions in the summer months. The through coaches to and from Lancashire had grown into a complete train which the Midland, under an agreement with the Lancashire and Yorkshire Railway, operated from Liverpool Exchange and Manchester Victoria to Glasgow and Edinburgh. The L. & Y. insisted that one of their second class carriages be included on this train even through it was in many ways less comfortable than the Midland's third class. Semi-fast trains between Leeds and Carlisle also carried through coaches from Lancashire as well as Bradford.

At night, a fascinating train was the 9.30 p.m. departure from St. Pancras which was made up of sleeping cars for Glasgow, Edinburgh, Dundee, Aberdeen, Perth and, in summer, Inverness. It divided at Leeds, where through carriages from Bristol were attached, while at Hellifield portions from Liverpool and Manchester were taken on. Other night trains were the 8.15 p.m. for Stranraer Harbour and Glasgow and the 12.00 midnight for Glasgow. Stranraer is close on a hundred miles distant from the termination of Midland metals at Carlisle, but by some skilful manoeuvring the company managed to acquire a share in a single line railway running through the southern part of Galloway. They took full advantage of the fact that they were able to offer a direct service from London to the Scottish terminal of the shortest sea route to Ireland. Eventually the Portpatrick and Wigtownshire Joint Committee was formed and the rail and harbour facilities at both Stranraer and Larne were substantially improved.

The onset of the 1914–18 war immediately brought a drastic reduction in services and nine years later the grouping saw both the Midland and the London and North-Western swallowed up into the London, Midland and Scottish Railways. The two deadly rivals were now partners and trains that had been run merely for the sake of competition were obsolete. In the 1930s, however, there were considerable improvements, and once again three expresses were running each way, daily, covering the 309 miles from St. Pancras to

Carlisle in just over 6 hours. The morning trains to and from Glasgow and Edinburgh were named respectively the 'Thames–Clyde' and 'Thames–Forth'. There was also a morning express from Leeds to Glasgow, with a through Edinburgh coach, to which a Manchester portion was added at Hellifield. In the reverse direction there were independent evening trains from both Edinburgh and Glasgow to Leeds, while the Manchester coach was attached to the St. Pancras train.

By the early 1970s the pattern was on a greatly reduced scale. The mid-day trains had ceased to operate, and the 'Thames–Forth' express re-christened the 'Waverley' had disappeared from the timetable following the closure of the Waverley Route in January, 1969. The 'Thames–Clyde', by now un-named, no longer ran non-stop from Leeds to Carlisle, but called at Skipton, Hellifield, Settle and Appleby. From St. Pancras to Carlisle took 6 hr. 51 min. compared with 6 hr. 20 min. at the turn of the century. There was only one night train – to Glasgow – and the only other regular express over the line was the morning train from Sheffield to Glasgow which had a counter-balancing working in the early evening. Glasgow services ran into Central instead of St. Enoch station. In 1977 there was some improvement when the service was re-cast, but at the same time a tenuous link with the Midland's glorious past finally disappeared when St. Pancras ceased to be a terminus for any Settle–Carlisle trains. Nottingham became the starting point for the revised services, with two through trains each way to Glasgow Central and one to Carlisle. North of the 'Border City' the main train of the day was routed over the electrified West Coast line instead of the great way round via Dumfries, giving an overall Nottingham–Glasgow time of 6 hrs. 1 min. – over half an hour faster than that achieved by the Midland in its golden age. An additional improvement was that for the first time for many years it became possible to make a day return journey from Carlisle to Leeds, although on the debit side night services over the line were finally withdrawn.

Local services were withdrawn on May 5th, 1970, on the closure of all stations on the line except Settle and Appleby. In their case before the North Western Area of the Transport Users' Consultative Committee, British Railways claimed that only 43 people regularly used the service which brought in an annual revenue of £9,000, compared with an expenditure of £61,000 a year. In its report to the Minister of Transport, the T.U.C.C. stated that the closure would cause severe or very severe hardship to local people, as well as considerable inconvenience and in some cases hardship to travellers from areas beyond the line who used the stations for access to the Yorkshire Dales National Park for holidays and the like. The Committee concluded that it could not suggest any means of alleviating this hardship, but the minister nevertheless approved closure. The Hawes branch was closed in 1959 and the track has been lifted.

In winter, the peace which pervades Mallerstang and Dentdale on Sunday can be unexpectedly shattered when a procession of trains scurries over Ais Gill. The reason is that the former London and North-Western line over Shap is periodically closed to enable engineering work to be undertaken and the Settle–Carlisle forms the logical diversion route – indeed it is now the only one, apart from that via Barrow and Whitehaven.

Dalesrail has provided its own novel form of passenger service, with a monthly week-end service during the tourist season and a special occasion for shoppers just before Christmas. Using DMUs, the service catered for upwards of 500 people on one Sunday alone during its most popular phase.

Goods Traffic

THE MIDLAND recovered some of its costs by operating goods trains even before the line was complete from Settle to Carlisle. When the southern part was ready, limestone could be despatched from the Craven Quarry, near Langcliffe, to the 'iron districts' near Bradford. Lime was also being used for 'plastering, fluxing, bleaching and agricultural purposes.'

The quarry company installed an immense Hoffman kiln, in which the continuous burning of limestone was possible. The lime was stacked within the kiln as blocks; coal was fed from above – having been raised to the level of the top of the kiln using water, entering and leaving a tank, as a counterweight – and in due course there was a siding and a dock beside the kiln. Men collected the burnt lime in wheelbarrows, trundled these up planks which had been set above the railway wagons, and when loading had taken place a train was ushered on to the main line.

It was mainly to speed goods from England to Scotland that the Settle–Carlisle came into being; local traffic was of lesser importance. As goods traffic began, nine trains were routed each way per day, quite apart from specials, and on Tuesdays and Fridays there was a pick-up train from Bradford to Appleby. Three times a week, special trains were arranged for cattle and sheep.

Early in 1876, it was noted: 'A large number of cattle and sheep are being sent into this district from Scotland, and the two companies – the North British and the Glasgow and South Western – send all their trade by the Midland route, as this line affords them a through route for their traffic destined south, and they are no longer under the power of the London and North-Western Railway, who always gave preference to the Caledonian traffic, detaining and delaying any that came by either of the other sources.'

That same year, the new goods station at Carlisle was said to cover 80 acres of land, 'and comprises Engine Sheds, Goods Warehouses, Cattle Docks, Marshalling Sidings, &c.' Sidings at Blea Moor permitted the shunting of the slower goods trains and allowed for the unimpeded passage of express passenger trains. Warehouses were provided at the most important stations.

Virtually every station had its cattle docks for the assembly of local stock, much of it purchased at an auction mart or other point of sale on land close to the railway, as at Lazonby and Ribblehead. Mr James Pratt, of Hawes, went into Scotland for his cows. Local farmers collected the stock from the station or employed a drover like Tommy Byker of Garsdale. The cattle usually arrived on a late train, and it was not unknown for Tommy to walk them through the night. All the surplus local farmstock went by rail, a special train leaving Hawes for Manchester each Monday evening. In October, when the large sheep sales took place, more specials were needed. Most of the dalesfolk converted their surplus milk into butter or cheese, but a number, having contracts with milkmen in towns, drove the laden kits to the nearest station with horse and float.

John Delaney became something of a tycoon when, sensing the importance of the railway to the commercial life of the area, he opened up the Beecroft quarry at Horton-in-Ribblesdale and had sidings installed. The railway brought him coal, and it took away his lime, in trucks on which his name was presented in the largest possible letters. Coal agents at various stations received coal and arranged for its local distribution. The opening of quarries created employment and provided an alternative to the harsh hill-farming.

In due course, anhydrite workings were opened south of Cumwhinton and Long Meg gave her name to a gypsum mine. The early miners ignored the 'blue cobble' which encased the gypsum, yet that 'cobble' was calcium sulphate, and during the 1939–45 war several industrial companies banded together to mine it. The rock was transported by rail to Widnes. Railway sidings were installed at Long Meg, and over perhaps 20 years some 2 million tons of 'blue cobble' passed over the Settle–Carlisle. (Long after the war, when the Widnes plant was in need of extensive repair, the Long Meg mine was closed; sulphur was by now easily obtainable elsewhere).

In the railway days, Hawes had a curious frontier flavour. The station belonged to the Midland, but was staffed by the North-Eastern, who also worked most of the trains through to Garsdale. Separate accounts were kept for each company. In the old days, thousands of flagstones, slates and building stones were consigned from Wensleydale quarries by rail. (Goods services were withdrawn from the Wensleydale branch in 1964; the metals were lifted and the track is now grassed over).

Off the Rails

THE GLAMOUR of any railway line centres on the trains, yet in a sense they are only accessories. Many less imposing facts on a rail system can easily be overlooked – until an accident occurs, happily a rare event, when we are suddenly made aware of the role of the signalman in maintaining a sense of order to the traffic.

The Settle–Carlisle was from the start fitted with block signalling equipment and interlocking points and levers. Wires to the distant signals were connected with apparatus that took up the slack if they expanded. Officials of the Midland were confident that this type of signal would not be overpowered by snow as had been those on the Great Northern, not long before. The Victorian signalmen used electrical instruments showing not only the position of the distant signals but whether or not the lamps were functioning. The old block system was to serve the line well down the years.

The two most notorious accidents on the Settle–Carlisle were in 1910 and 1913, on the wild upland stretches between Garsdale and Aisgill. The accident of Christmas Eve, 1910, was found to be due to negligence on the part of the signalman at Garsdale, which was then known as Hawes Junction. It was a wild day, with the wind bearing heavy showers of rain. Two light engines that had piloted two up-trains early that day waited for the signal that would permit then to return to Carlisle.

The signals were pulled off at 5.44 a.m., and the drivers of the light engines responded. In fact, the signals were for an express between St. Pancras and Glasgow (the signalman had overlooked the light engines on the main line when he accepted the express). As those engines came off the viaduct at Lunds, the express, which was double-headed, caught them up and ploughed into them at 65 miles an hour. The carriages of the express were gas-lit, and in the terrible blaze that followed the collision they were reduced to a heap of charred matchwood. (As a consequence of this accident, the Midland began extensive installation of track circuits on their main lines at all junctions of any importance).

Such an incident reflected badly on a signalman, but this was a rare blot on a record of conscientious service by generations of men who, manning such boxes at Blea Moor and Aisgill, had a job as lonely as any in England. For hours on end, they had only the sound of the curlew, and the sight of rain-laden clouds scudding off Whernside or Wild Boar Fell to keep them company. As an example of their dedication, it may be noted that Dick Clark, of Clapham, cycled to and from the box at Helwith Bridge for 19 years. Apart from the introduction of some colour light signals, the pattern altered little from the time the line was opened. (Many of the boxes have now been closed, and some – as at Helwith Bridge and Selside – actually removed).

Less than three years after the incident at Lunds Viaduct, on September 2, 1913, a sleeper from Glasgow and Stranraer to St. Pancras came to a stand half a mile north of Aisgill summit. The engine had run short of steam because of poor coal and the fact that no pilot had been available for the 243-ton train. The sleeper was being followed by a night train from Inverness and Edinburgh, the crew of which were also having footplate difficulties because of poor coal. They were so pre-occupied with trying to get sufficient steam that they over-ran the signals at Mallerstang and collided with the back of the stationary train. Fire broke out, and 14 people lost their lives. It was, as must be expected on the Settle–Carlisle, a wet and dark night, with, on this occasion, a strong wind blowing from the north-east.

Another tragedy occurred on January 19, 1918, and this time it was not caused by human error. A landslip occurred in Long Meg cutting, between Little Salkeld and Lazonby, immediately ahead of a daytime St. Pancras to Glasgow express. The driver had no chance to reduce speed, and the train plunged into the soggy clay at 60 miles an hour, telescoping the two leading coaches. Seven passengers were killed. A repetition of this tragedy was avoided only because of the vigilance of a driver passing through the cutting north of Dent Head. He noticed that the ground was bulging ominously and conveyed a warning.

The first accident of which we have details occurred on August 15, 1875, less than two weeks after the line was opened to goods traffic. Shortly after 12 noon, a 'peculiar oscillation of the engine' was felt as it passed by a cattle creep at Culgaith. Part of the line appeared to be giving way. There was some confusion about reporting the incident, and when the next train arrived the middle portion left the rails and crashed down the embankment on to the road below. The guard applied the handbrakes to the rear portion, but the engine and tender left the rails and became embedded in the embankment, carrying three wagons with them. Twenty other wagons were 'smashed almost to atoms,' and the contents strewn all over the road. The line was completely blocked.

In modern times, a serious accident occurred on January 11, 1960, when the driver of a 'Britannia' class locomotive working the

Glasgow to St. Pancras night express stopped at Garsdale to examine his engine, but did not notice that both the right hand slide-bars had dropped off. At Settle, the connecting rod finally fell away from the piston and ploughed into the track. A down goods train was derailed and struck the St. Pancras train, causing the death of five passengers.

In the winter of 1964, a consignment of cars was blown from a train. And throughout the period of operation, it was not uncommon for tarpaulins to be ripped off wagons at Ribblehead and be blown a mile or so away – a windfall in a literal sense for any farmer short of stack sheets!

Navvies at work in a cutting.

The Workforce

GENERATIONS of dedicated railwayfolk, living sparsely in remote areas, have ensured the smooth operation of the Settle–Carlisle. They were to remember in particular the extremes of climate. In the steam days, footplate men worked in pitifully exposed cabs, and station staff clambered up signals to replenish the fuel. Maintenance gangs were buffeted by the wind, and drenched by rain, as they attended to the permanent way, masons were chilled on the viaducts, and the tunnel gangs emerged from their shifts looking like miners. It needed a special form of dedication to be on shift duty at a remote signal box such as Blea Moor.

John Mason, who was employed at Hawes station for 48 years, retiring in 1948, remembered an instruction in the railway rule book – that a railway servant should be 'prompt, civil and obliging.' It was an instruction to which he responded when dealing with people, not only at work but in his daily life. Incidentally, John Mason began work at 15s. a week; he retired as porter-signalman with a wage of £5 2s. a week.

Hellifield, a few miles south of Settle Junction, and an important junction with the Lancashire and Yorkshire Railway (Lanky), was as shift-concious as a mining community. You could not wander through the village, by day or night, without seeing a railwayman either going to work or returning from it. A guard whose train encountered snowdrifts at Ais Gill returned to Hellifield 21 hungry and chilling hours later. The knocker-up made his doleful rounds, rapping on doors in the wee small hours and shouting 'Double-head to Carlisle' or 'Relief to Manchester.' If he added to his message '. . . and lodge' it meant that someone would spend a night away from home. Exceptionally long hours were worked by the crews of the snow ploughs that were quartered at Hellifield; the men were called upon whenever the Drag was overblown.

A contrasting community, Garsdale Head, was virtually all connected with the railway. There were 200 people here as recently as 1953, and old-timers remembered when the Methodist chapel near the Moorcock viaduct was packed. Evangelical services were spread over a week. Gone is the 200, volume library, the gift of a thoughtful lady passenger. A visitor no longer sees the 80,000 gallon tank from which water was supplied for thirsty locomotives. The Tank House was from the 1930s until the coming of television a centre for domino and whist drives, potato pie suppers and concerts. Some of the events in the Tank House raised up to £40 for the Bradford Royal Infirmary. A woman living in a cottage near Ais Gill was fond of recalling that she hung out her washing on the open ground nearby. Once she nearly trod on a pee-wit nest!

Railway work was considered secure. A man was carefully vetted and he had a temporary appointment for about two years before being given a permanent position. The temporary man received 2s. or so more than the regular employees. In the 1930s, a platelayer was given accommodation in one of the cottages in Salt Lake. He earned 31s.9d. with stoppages, which was an average wage for the district. 'The quarrymen earned a bit more.' Of the wage, the platelayer paid 5s.4d. in rent.

A man who was in the Blea Moor maintenance gang for 13 years lived during that time at one of the local cottages, not far from the signal box, and more than a mile from Ribblehead. Letters for Blea Moor were delivered by the Chapel-le-Dale postman, operating on foot. The family shopping was carried out in Settle, groceries being ordered – and delivered to Ribblehead station – once a month. From here, the groceries were transported to Blea Moor by the stopping freight train. This railwayman, a Methodist local preacher, often carried his bicycle across Ribblehead viaduct at the start of a journey to a local chapel, and when he was planned to preach at Dent he would carry it through Blea moor tunnel. He knew the times of the trains, and 'there was not much traffic on a Sunday.' His wife had more than once crossed the viaduct at Ribblehead with her baby in her arms when walking to Ribblehead, to catch a train for Settle.

With their smart uniforms, and air of considerable authority, the Settle–Carlisle stationmasters were much respected members of the community. When Mr Douglas Cobb was the stationmaster at Garsdale in 1953, he began to cultivate a platform garden. The gardening tradition was nowhere better demonstrated than at Horton-in-Ribblesdale, and later at Settle, when the stationmaster was Mr J. M. Taylor. A former stationmaster at Dent attempted to grow flowers and vegetables at an elevation of 1,155 feet. He also kept an eye on the line for trespassing sheep, and told us: 'Any sheep that are knocked down by a train are always the best in the flock. There's never a bad one among them!'

Bill Sharpe was one of those who served as stationmaster at Ribblehead and also ran the local weather station. Mr Sharpe entered railway service in 1949, after local farm work, and his career reflected the vagaries of the Settle–Carlisle. He was porter, signalman, stationmaster, area assistant manager (for a month) and then became relief signalman. Incidentally, Ribblehead became a weather station in 1938, but it was not until 1954 that a rain gauge was installed.

The driver of a steam locomotive was invariably a character. Ernest Jarvis, of Skipton, recalls a protracted journey in the winter of 1947: 'We signed on to work the 5.45 p.m. fiom Skipton to Garsdale, where we had to pick up a train. It started to snow. I'd only half a tank of water, but it was enough to take me to Blea Moor, where I could fill up. They stopped me at Ribblehead. The Leeds man was coming up behind, and he hadn't any water. I said: "Neither have I, owd lad." They said: "It saves a block." I said: "I don't care what it's going to save; in t'long run it's going to lose." I hadn't to go until the Leeds man arrived. So he came.

'According to his water gauge, he'd more water than I had. Remember, I set off from Skipton with half a tank, and that was at 5.45 p.m. Now it was eight o'clock the next morning. It had taken some time, and I'd climbed up half a dozen posts in purpose to see whether pegs were up or not! When we got to Garsdale – eventually – they dug us out of snow to let us go across to let this Leeds man come before us. They couldn't get points up so they had to let us go first.

'Our train, a munition train from the Hawes branch, was in a layby, with a brake at each end. They got facing points up, but the trailing points wouldn't come. They'd reckoned that when I trailed through them, they'd shut, squeezing out the snow. We got inside – nearly – except for four wheels of the engine! In the meantime, the guard had taken the back brake off and was just climbing out of the front brake next to the engine. He shoved us a bit, so they had to let us go.

'That's when I walked straight off the vans into Mallerstang box. You couldn't see no Mallerstang valley. I asked the signalman how he was going on for a relief, and he told me it was his third day at the box. "How is tha going on for grub, then?" "They're sending it up." I said: "Oh, we'll have a share wi' thee". He said: "You can have what you like." So we had some sandwiches and a couple o' Oxo cubes and some snow water, and that were that!

'The two snow ploughs from Hellifield were at Kirkby Stephen, moving backards and forrards to fill up with watter. There was no room for two roads. Eventually they came thrusting up. The inspector, Bert Minn – a grand, understanding chap – said: "Na then, how are you going on?" I says: "In t'muck." To tell you the truth, the gauge was out. We had 500 gallons more than what the gauge said. The inspector asked me if I'd enough water for Appleby. I said: "Yes – to tell you the honest gospel truth, if there's nowt on t'road we've enough there for Appleby. Course, we'll have nowt to throw away."

'So they let us go before the ploughs, on condition we did not pick up any water at Kirkby Stephen. The Leeds man was well back –

Sherwood Viaduct.

Aisgill, or somewhere. So at Appleby, my fireman went looking for some food, and he came back with 12 meat pies in a flour bag (they hadn't t'sense to empty t'flour out of it), a packet of cigarettes, half an ounce of thin twist (for me) and a box of matches. He must have been away for an hour. The signalman shouts: "Are you about right now?" I said: "Just about, old lad, but give us time to put a shovel in the fire-oil and warm up some pies." I had two pies. The fireman scoffed the rest.

'We landed at the main line, Durranhill, and I remember laughing at my fireman, wi' his black face. Think on, it was mid-day, the day after we had started. The inspector gave us three cheers. They all cheered. It seems we were the first train to get through from the south for three days. The passenger trains had come over t'Nor-west, by Ingleton.

'Somebody said: "Control wants you." I said: "They're a bit late in t'day, aren't they?" We were told to book on at Kingsmoor, but I didn't want to go there. Last time it happened they were puncturing fish tins to see if there were any fit to eat. We'd go into town, for a wash and brush up – we looked like two chimney sweeps – then we'd go to find the most high-class restaurant we could find!

'We heard an express was going from Citadel, on the Nor-west line. We got into t'first coach – and afore it got to Lowgill I was fast asleep. We signed off at a quarter to six. That wasn't a bad do, was it? Though I've had even worse times – down t'pits!'

A Carlisle man who began work on the railway at Durranhill in 1917 – when he was 15 years old – told me that his first 'firing' job was with Bob Newbould, who was a main line driver aged 73. This man also recalled the vulnerability of the old-time footplate men to the weather. When the Helm Wind blew, it plucked coal from the fireman's shovel. He had to wait until the train entered a cutting before he could replenish the fire.

Of the guards, a Hellifield man related how joyful he was when he became a guard during the 1939–45 war. His railway career, like those of others, had been blighted by the years of industrial depression. He had been redundant as a ticket collector at Heysham in 1932, and was a temporary guard at Colne for four years before moving to Hellifield. He retired, after 43 years service, with a railway pension of half-a-guinea a week. He could have 'stopped on', but after 43 years 'I'd had enough.' He kept a railway whistle as a sole tangible link with his railway service, and yet he was always proud to recall his service on the Settle–Carlisle.

It is said that a guard on a goods train during the 1939–45 war was somewhat unfamiliar with the route, as his behaviour indicated to the driver within a few miles. The train departed from Hellifield, and at Settle that driver had to stop because it appeared the brake on the guard's van had been applied. The guard eventually confessed that he had not often travelled the Settle–Carlisle. When asked how he knew when to apply the brake, he said: 'I've four ball bearings. I chuck 'em on t'floor. If they go that way, we're going uphill, and if they go t'other way it's downhill!'

John Mason, who has already been mentioned, was born four years after the line to Hawes was opened, and he worked at Hawes station from 1900 until his retirement. He remembered when pride

A Pullman coach.

was everywhere evident. The station staff kept the buildings tidy, and the locomen made their engines shine through frequent cleaning. 'I've known a fireman leave the footplate as soon as he reached Hawes so that he could polish the brass work and clean and oil other sections of the engine. In those days, a man used a certain locomotive for most of his railway career.' Starting as a lad porter, Mr Mason was on duty at 5.45 a.m. to fill the foot pans that warmed the compartments of a passenger train. Paraffin lamps (later gas lamps) provided the illumination. He clambered along the roofs of the carriages, lifting small lids to ignite the gas.

Station bookstalls were presided over by men of undoubted character. A man who began as a boy at the bookstall of W. H. Smith's, aged 13, received 2s.6d. a week. In summer, two boys were employed by the manager, one boy delivering newspapers and magazines in the village, and the other carrying a basket full of periodicals to passengers when the trains stopped for a few minutes. This man then started work at the refreshment room for the same wage. A manageress, three waitresses, a cook and cellarman were on the staff of the refreshment room at that time. Luncheon baskets were available to passengers. He began work at 7 a.m., hauling a large four-wheeled barrow along the platforms to collect dirty trays and pots, which were then washed up, using a large bath.

Harry Cox, who worked on the line before the 1914–18 war, used to recall the type of cabin built by men engaged in viaduct or tunnel work; it was entirely home-made from such materials as railway sleepers. Men even made their own seats. The foreman would knock up a rough cupboard in which he could keep his papers. The fireplace extended into the room, and was adorned by a metal plate on which food was warmed. The fireman allowed a man to go to the cabin an hour before 'bait' time to prepare the food, which was commonly 'half a collop of bacon and a couple of eggs.'

The men of the tunnel maintenance gang occupied a gloomy world. The first 400 yards at the southern end of Blea Moor tunnel is on a curve, and anyone working from that end soon lost sight of the friendly blob of daylight which was the tunnel mouth. A man who was with the Blea Moor gang from 1933 until 1946 remembered when the men carried tin duck lamps that gave off a considerable amount of smoke, but these were preferable to the lighting units used earlier – naptha lamps, which were prone to burst into flames. In the steam days, smoke from a passing train might reduce visibility to zero, and it was especially dense when double-headed trains were passing. A man moving in thick smoke kept to the prescribed course by tapping a stick on the edge of the rail. The life-expectancy of a rail in the sulphur-ridden tunnel was about 10 years, or half that of a rail laid in the open. The rails were, for a time, painted, in an attempt to prolong their working lives.

Run-down – and Revival

'ON THE BASIS of the undoubted hardship that closure of the line would cause, together with the strength of the commercial case presented for its retention, we strongly and emphatically recommend that consent to British Rail's proposal to close the Settle – Carlisle line be refused.' These resounding words form the conclusion to the Joint Report of the North East and North West England Transport Users' Consultative Committees, submitted to the Transport Secretary on December 12th, 1986. On the same day British Rail made its own submission to the Minister, arguing that its closure plans were fully justified – annual revenue from the line amounted to £1m compared with costs of almost £2m. In addition, £5m needed to be spent immediately, much of it on Ribblehead viaduct, and £15m over the next few years on resignalling, replacing worn-out double tracks with a single high-speed line and repairing three other viaducts. Just two months later it was announced that from May 1987 the line was to have its greatest-ever density of daytime Leeds – Carlisle services – five trains each way on weekdays and two on Sundays.

This mixture of gloom and optimism, despair and enterprise, has characterised the last decade in which the Settle – Carlisle has more and more become the focus of public attention. The first real piece of innovation came in 1975 with the instantly successful launching of *Dalesrail,* promoted by the Yorkshire Dales National Park Committee and involving the co-operation of Cumbria County Council, British Rail and the National Bus Company. The first move was to carry out repair and improvement works at Horton-in-Ribblesdale, Ribblehead, Dent, Garsdale and Kirkby Stephen stations, which had been closed for almost five years, to enable them to be re-opened on an occasional basis. This paved the way for the National Park Committee to charter a diesel unit which on five week-ends in the summer of 1975 worked a return service from Leeds and Appleby on the Sunday, stopping at Settle and the re-opened stations. The fare structure was designed positively to encourage visitors to travel into the National Park by rail instead of road, and as additional attractions guided walks were provided from several of the stations and connecting bus services arranged from

Garsdale to Sedbergh and the Hawes area. The same pattern was followed on the Saturday, except that an additional return service was operated so that local residents, long deprived of public transport facilities, could have a day out in Leeds. The service has become a regular feature, and has been extended to Carlisle with the re-opening of stations at Langwathby, Lazonby and Armathwaite. *Dalesrail* trains from East Lancashire have also been developed, calling at the normally-closed Clitheroe station on the Blackburn – Hellifield line.

In 1976 the centenary of the opening of the Settle – Carlisle was celebrated in fine style. Hopes that British Rail might allow the various special trains to be steam-hauled were not realised, but two steam locomotives – *Hardwicke* and *Flying Scotsman* – were permitted to run to the southern end of the line at Settle. Two years later, B.R. changed its policy and agreed to a limited return of steam specials over the route. Then, in the early months of 1980, thanks to the tireless efforts of the Steam Locomotive Operators' Association, the Cumbrian Mountain Express was introduced with steam haulage from Skipton to Carlisle and Carnforth to Skipton, the electrified West Coast main line completing the circular tour. Such workings have understandably proved an enduring success.

Optimism was suddenly deflated early in 1981 when the bombshell broke that Ribblehead viaduct was deteriorating to such an extent that it would either have to be replaced within as little as five years or the line closed. The next move came later the same year when it was announced that the Settle & Carlisle's Inter City service – comprising three Nottingham–Glasgow trains each way daily – was to be diverted via Manchester and Preston and replaced by two Leeds–Carlisle 'locals'. British Rail insisted it was 'entirely a commercial decision', but there were many allegations of 'dirty tricks' and 'closure by stealth'. Leaked documents subsequently proved that this was exactly what was happening: a deliberate policy was being pursued of removing traffic so that it could be claimed the line was not needed. Surely, the argument ran, there could be no case for replacing Ribblehead Viaduct at a cost approaching £6 million if the railway was not essential as a through route.

These moves were a factor leading to the formation of the Friends of the Settle–Carlisle Line, but despite their protests and those of the railway unions, Members of Parliament and the Transport Users' Consultative Committee, the proposed changes were implemented at the start of the new timetable in May 1982. Buffet car expresses were replaced by pathetic four-coach formations running to schedules that seemed to have been designed to be as slow and inconvenient as possible.

It took only another twelve months for the planned run-down to be completed with the diversion of all through freight traffic to other routes, a move that created extra mileage and caused high-speed services to be disrupted while Settle & Carlisle signalmen sat for hours on end without a train in sight. Paranoia set in with British Rail determined at all costs to retain its stance that the tracks over Ais Gill were surplus to requirements. When the new freight arrangements were introduced, a goods that had got as far as Skipton was actually turned back! Light engines northbound for Carlisle were sent round via Carnforth and the edict went out that the line was not to be used for diversionary purposes. For many winters it had been the practice on Sundays for West Coast main line services to be routed over the Settle & Carlisle in the morning and early afternoon so that essential engineering work could take place. This came to an end with the winter 1984/85 timetable, prepared in 1983, which revealed a sorry state of affairs. Virtually the whole of Cumbria became a railway desert, passengers southbound from Carlisle having to face a 2½ hour bus journey to Preston or wait until the first train of the day to Euston at the decidedly late hour of 3.45 pm. Northbound, the morning Liverpool–Glasgow service made a massive detour via York and Newcastle.

In many ways, British Rail overdid it. Had the whole approach looked rather less deceitful, the opposition to the inevitable closure announcement in August 1983 might not have been quite so determined. BR's case was that withdrawal of passenger services, enabling the tracks to be lifted north of Ribblehead quarry and south of Appelby, would bring a net annual saving of £1.5 million and a total saving in capital expenditure of £6.7 million – mainly on Ribblehead viaduct. Hardly had these figures been released than there was a further leaking of documents, showing that BR had 'adjusted' the budget by increasing the cost of diesel fuels by 250 per cent and diesel locomotive maintenance by a staggering 450 per cent.

The next step was for British Rail to publish a formal closure notice, giving objectors six weeks to make representations to the TUCC at York or Manchester. This it did in December 1983, by a supreme irony on the same day that it was forced to divert West Coast main line services over the route as the result of a severe derailment. It was but the first of several embarrassments, for under the threat of legal action it was conceded that users of Dales Rail and steam-hauled excursions were also eligible to object and therefore the notices were re-issued. Then it was pointed out that the Newcastle TUCC could also hear objections – and so the whole procedure had to be gone through for a third time!

In order to challenge the B.R. case, Cumbria County Council took the initiative in bringing together the relevant local authorities and tourist boards to sponsor a £30,000 independent report on the future of the line by the planning and economic consultants PEIDA. Published in the summer of 1984, it put the whole by now emotive

Motive Power
Steam Age to Diesel

Steam encounters diesel at Appleby in June 1967. *(Derek Cross)*

Freight motive power in steam days. Above: 4F 0-6-0 No. 44451 at Ais Gill in July 1961 – note the gypsy-style caravan on the well wagon. Below: Britannia No. 70014 'Iron Duke' takes water at Appleby in April 1967. *(Derek Cross)*

Above: Failed and relief locomotives at Armathwaite on June 3rd, 1967 – ex-Crosti boilered 9F 2-10-0 No. 92025 and 5MT No. 44675.   Below: 5MT No. 44892 trundles north across Ais Gill viaduct in June 1967. *(Derek Cross)*

The L.N.E.R. influence. Top: D20 No. 62347 arrives at Garsdale with a two-coach local from Northallerton and Hawes. *(J. W. Armstrong)* Bottom: A3 No. 60082 'Neil Gow' leaves Appleby in June 1961 with a Glasgow–Leeds train. For a relatively brief period prior to dieselisation, members of this class which had been displaced from the East Coast main line took over most of the passenger workings on the Settle–Carlisle. *(Derek Cross)*

Top: On summer Saturdays in 1967, the morning Leeds–Glasgow relief was regularly steam-hauled by Jubilee No. 45562 'Alberta' and attracted a great following from enthusiasts. Here it pauses at Carlisle Citadel on August 26th. Bottom: A forerunner of steam specials to come. No. 7029 'Clun Castle' passes Durran Hill Junction, Carlisle, in October 1967. (*Derek Cross*)

Diesel power in the Eden Valley. This page: 45052 near Baron Wood in July 1980 with a Glasgow–Nottingham express. *(G. W. Morrison)*

Top: Lazonby village and church provide an attractive backcloth to 47051 heading south in February 1982. **Bottom:** Inter-City 125 HST near Armathwaite on a photographic outing for BR Publicity in October 1981. *(G. W. Morrison)*

40079 sneaks into view at Selside with a northbound freight on July 11th, 1979. *(G. W. Morrison)*

The back cover photographs show (top) 5MT No. 44675 at Ais Gill in 1965 *(Derek Cross)* **and Class 47 No. 47478 at Kirkby Stephen in 1981** *(G. W. Morrison).*

Settle & Carlisle debate on a factual footing. Although describing B.R.'s policy towards the line as one of 'wanton neglect', it nevertheless in several ways fudged the real issues. It was rather more optimistic about Ribblehead viaduct, and yet failed to make a detailed appraisal of the various repair options. It conceded that closure would impose a high social cost but neither analysed this in detail nor made its own assessment of figures claimed by B.R. It showed that it would cost virtually as much to close the line as to keep it open with enhanced revenue, and yet finally left the ball firmly in the government's court by stating that it would be unrealistic for B.R. to maintain existing operations in view of the high financial considerations. Not surprisingly, the report was seen by both British Rail and the closure opponents as vindicating their case.

In order to achieve better co-ordination, the Friends had in the meantime joined with Transport 2000 and the Railway Development Society to form the Settle - Carlisle Railway Joint Action Committee, which late in 1984 broke new ground in the area of opposition to rail closures by deciding to become a limited company with fulltime staff and a proposed annual budget of £55,000. Over the next year the campaign really took off so that by the end of the statutory period the number of objectors to the closure totalled a quite unprecedented 22,265 people - and one dog! The Action Committee commissioned TEST (Transport and Environment Studies) to make a detailed appraisal of possible additional services - its report published early in 1986 advocated further local workings between Skipton and Carlisle; a 'figure-of-eight' service taking in Leeds, Manchester, Preston, Blackburn, Hellifield and Carnforth; and, most importantly, an Inter-City 125 High Speed Train link from Leeds and Bradford to Glasgow.

A curious twist to the closure saga had come with the appointment in 1983 of a Project Manager for the Settle - Carlisle line. The first B.R. post of its kind, it involved overseeing not just the smooth running of the closure process but also marketing the line in order to maximise revenue during the period leading up to abandonment. The surprising choice for the post was one of B.R.'s most controversial marketing men, Ron Cotton - inventor of the Saver ticket. His flair brought such an upsurge in passengers that the two regular trains soon extended from four to as many as eleven coaches - and even then additional workings had to be scheduled. British Rail found itself in the curious position of going into the TUCC closure hearings in the spring of 1986 with the line enjoying the best growth rate in its Provincial Sector.

The hearings, occupying a marathon sixteen days, heard evidence from British Rail and almost 400 users including over a hundred representing a vast diversity of corporate bodies. There was much criticism of the proposed alternative service from Leeds to Carlisle via Carnforth, where passengers would be left to admire the surroundings of the Down Goods Loop for over half an hour while awaiting a path over the West Coast main line. Severe doubts were also cast on the prospects for alternative bus services, particularly between Penrith and Appleby. Claims that the Settle - Carlisle formed an essential part of the national heritage came thick and fast. For example, the Council for the Protection of Rural England roundly concluded its evidence: 'The case for closure should not hinge on either hardship or the future economic viability of a line which British Rail regard as surplus to requirements. What in effect is Britain's longest ancient monument also affords the opportunity to view one of the most beautiful parts of England. Applying economic rationale to the line is as irrelevant as it would be if applied to the two other "great wonders of northern England" with which it has been compared – Hadrian's Wall and York Minster. The Settle & Carlisle has to be seen as an important and unique part of our heritage and not just another redundant railway'.

In their wide-ranging report the TUCCs accused British Rail of an 'apparent lack of candour' over their intentions for the line; found that residents of Settle and especially Appleby would suffer severe hardship in gaining access to Leeds and Carlisle; condemned the proposed alternative services; and suggested the 'the linchpin of the future prosperity of the area was largely dependent on the line's continuance'. The Committees concluded that the Settle - Carlisle had a positive future with its full potential yet to be tapped, and that there was 'an overwhelmingly strong case' for its retention.

The period between the hearings and publication of the report did in fact see a bold move to increase traffic. With the aid of an initial one-year subsidy of £72,500 from various local authorities, a regular *Dalesman* service of two trains each way between Skipton and Carlisle, stopping at stations previously only served by *Dalesrail,* was inaugurated on July 14th, 1986. In addition some of the existing Leeds - Carlisle trains now made extra stops at certain of these stations. Further enterprise saw the introduction of a mini-bus service from Sedbergh and Hawes to Garsdale station, so that for example it was possible to leave the Wensleydale market town at 9.50 am and be in Carlisle for a day's shopping just 1¾ hours later.

These developments paved the way for the 1987 service with most of the five-each-way trains calling at the re-opened intermediate stations. Ron Cotton, the man appointed to oversee the closure of England's most spectacular main line, had in four years seen its revenue quadruple and its services more than double. Described by one industrial commentator as B.R.'s 'UFO' who senior management pretended did not exist, he saw the new timetable through to the point where it could not be rescinded and then quietly took early retirement.

Victorian Pride

OUR TALE IS TOLD. Now we might usefully remind ourselves of the spirit of those who imposed a sophisticated transport system on a wilderness. When the Settle–Carlisle came into use, Britain was at the peak of its industrial might, being the workshop of the world. There was general pride in any new manifestation of British inventiveness and skill. Towards the end of 1874, as work on the Settle–Carlisle was drawing to its close, 'Rambler' toured the line, jotting down his impressions in a series of newspaper articles.

He wrote jauntily, marvelling at features every mile of the way; quickening the pulses of his readers by stories of the navvies and the Pennine weather. In one recent prolonged rainy spell, carters who operated a shuttle system between local coal pits and the 'Moorcock', near Garsdale – the coal was needed for a variety of engines – 'took their pay and were discharged' rather than face the miserable weather. One night, a steam 'traveller' was blown off Arten Gill viaduct and the storm demolished an engine shed at Garsdale Head.

The Settle–Carlisle was largely a rural line, and our correspondent noted that 'no mill chimneys will be seen after passing Langcliffe until the Carlisle chimneys shall come into view.' Soon he had reached the head of the dale, commenting that 'the railway works on the moorlands north and south of Blea Moor are in one of the wildest, windiest, coldest and dreariest localities in the north of England.' But enough of the weather. There was cheer in many of the huts erected for the navvies on and around Batty Green. 'After work the soberest portion of the men wash and make themselves tidy, then sit down to a good and savoury supper, and afterwards either take to reading or form themselves into a mixed choir of instrumental and vocal music.'

Engineers provided him with facts and figures about the main features of the line. 'Between the Ingleton road bridge and Batty Moss (later Ribblehead) viaduct there is an immense embankment of limestone ballast, containing 200,000 cubic yards . . . The cubical contents of the viaduct are 33,000 yards, and it is computed that over 1,500,000 bricks (all locally made) have been used in the arches . . . Some idea of the magnificent character of the viaduct may be formed when it is stated that the black limestone of Blea Moor or Little Dale quarries has been used in as large blocks as could be got, some of which weigh from 7 to 8 tons.' Workmen were still busy in Blea Moor tunnel, though some 1,000 yards of single permanent way had been laid. 'When completed, this long subterranean iron way will be arched its whole length on account of the rock being liable to spontaneous explosions.'

Everywhere, the engineers triumphed over nature. North of Blea Moor, becks tumbled from the heights and had to be accommodated in culverts. Then there was the Dee, 'or black river, from its source being in the peat moors. It is only a small stream excepting in a rainy season, and then at times it swells to such a desolating extent as witnessed a few years ago, when bridges, walls, macadamised roads, trees, land and stones were carried down with terrible force.' Pride in the line was everywhere evident. 'It may be remarked that the portion of the line from Batty Green to the northern end of Black Moss (later Rise Hill) tunnel, for its massive works of masonry and the scenery which bounds it on both sides, occupies almost an unrivalled position among the great iron ways of England.'

Dandry Mire, where an embankment was intended, swallowed virtually everything that was tipped there over a space of three years, and so a viaduct was planned. 'Every inducement is held out to good masons to push on the structure to completion. There is no limit to working hours, at one shilling per hour.' The contractors, Messrs Benton and Woodiwiss, also had a care for the wellbeing of off-duty workmen, even tramps. 'In connection with the school at Garsdale is a coffee-room, in which coffee is supplied at the contractor's expense. If bread and butter should be required, that is also given . . . The coffee-room has been a great advantage to many of the men, who in summer made it a home during the day, and then at night slept in some outhouse, and thus saved the expense of lodgings.'

'Rambler' enthused about the substantial nature of the buildings. At Kirkby Stephen, the station was being constructed 'according to that mixed style of architecture adopted by the Midland Company. It will comprise ladies' and gentlemen's waiting rooms, waiting hall and shed, stationmaster's office, porters' room, &c . . . The stationmaster's house will be on a plan which is a great improvement on the old style. It will consist of seven rooms, a spacious entrance, and staircase.' Our traveller stood on Smardale viaduct, a 'lofty structure', and described the views. 'On the east, the Nine Standards and neighbouring hills, on the north east the Pennine Range, on the south east the Ravenstonedale mountains and the water running down a cleft in Green Bell Hill from the farthest source of the Lune, with all the rich lands and woods in the valley . . .' The fine slopes in Scandal Gill 'was a painting befitting the terminus of the second contract.'

'Rambler' acknowledged a certain nobility in the navvy's character, but was much aware of some of his vices. 'Bad weather, roving workmen, and boulder clay have seriously retarded operations on the second contract, but drink has been the gigantic hindrance. The manager said that in 90 per cent of the huts drink was sold, and that neither policemen nor supervisors would help to check the illicit trade.'

Cuttings, some of considerable depth, are major features of the Settle–Carlisle that today are little noticed. To 'Rambler', they were another testimony of the Victorian spirit, and an idication that not only faith will move mountains. At Crosby Garrett, the cutting shouted to be noticed, a 'work of patient and persevering labour . . . This immense gorge in the rocks has a very imposing aspect from rail level, and no one can walk through it without feeling that it has been a work of great magnitude.' This cutting is 374 yards long, and with a maximum depth of 56 feet. Crowhill Cutting also impressed our writer, being 792 yards in length and 46 feet in the deepest place. 'Its cubical contents are 218,523 yards.'

Materials taken from the cuttings were dumped handily, as embankments. 'Rambler', on his 1874 journey, noticed that some of the embankments, where the permanent way had been laid 'had sustained much damage from the excessive rains. In some places the ground had so far slipped that the metals were propped up with large stones to make them passable for the locomotives. The doing of work from the same cause over and over again has swallowed a large item of the money spent on the Settle and Carlisle line.'

When railway engineers disturbed the ground, they looked for stone of sufficiently high quality to be used for building. At Appleby, 'Rambler' was told that stone dug out of the cuttings was not suitable for building purposes. Stone for the one-arch skew bridge that was set in the ponderous embankment of Battlebarrow had been transported from Dufton quarries, two and a half miles away. Much stone was needed, for the bridge had heavy retaining walls 'to sustain the pressure of the superincumbent earth.' Bricks provided the lining, 'with stone arch quoins.' At Battlebarrow, the cubical contents of the embankment were 253,000 yards; not far to the north 231,665 cubic yards of material was removed from Crackanthorpe or Plump Cutting, 'a heavy rock . . . attended with some difficulty on account of slips.'

At Long Marton, foundations had been laid for a large goods yard, 'and a heavy work of excavation had been done in diverting the highway.' Our writer was astonished by the dramatic succession of cuttings and embankments as the railway entered its final phase. He marvelled at the Victorian drive and enterprise, and at the ability of the contractors to muster men, horses and material. Contract No. 3, though away from the high fells, demanded 1,500 men, 90 horses and six locomotives.

In succeding years, maintaining the railway in such fierce conditions was to demand the pluck and tenacity shown by those who had constructed it . . .

The Main Structures

Ribblehead Viaduct. 24 spans, 440 yards long, with maximum height of about 100 feet. Construction period between 1870 and 1875. The piers extend from the rock some 25 feet below ground level.

Blea Moor Tunnel. 2,629 yards long, maximum depth below the moor top of 500 feet. Three ventilation shafts. Was being excavated between 1870 and 1875.

Dent Head Viaduct. 10 spans, 197 yards long, maximum height of 100 feet. At elevation of 1,150 feet. Of limestone construction.

Arten Gill Viaduct. 11 spans, 220 yards in length, 117 feet high. Arches turned with stone, not brick. Was constructed of the local limestone, a dark, highly fossilised stone known locally as 'marble'. Excavations to depth of over 50 feet for some of the piers.

Rise Hill Tunnel. 1,213 yards in length. Two ventilation shafts, the deepest being 147 feet. This tunnel was originally known as Black Moss.

Dandry Mire. 12 spans, 227 yards long, 50 feet high. This viaduct was built in desperation; it had originally been intended to make an embankment.

Aisgill Viaduct. 4 spans, 87 yards long, 75 feet high. At elevation of 1,167 feet above sea level.

Birkett Tunnel. 424 yards long. The line in this tunnel has a considerable gradient, 1 in 100.

Smardale Viaduct. 12 spans, 237 yards long, 130 feet high. A limestone structure over Scandal Beck. The piers rest on rock, some of them at a depth below the stream bed of 45 feet.

Crosby Garrett Viaduct. 6 spans, 110 yards long, 55 feet high. Crosses part of the village after which it is named.

Griseburn Viaduct. 7 spans, 142 yards long, 74 feet high. Spans the Potts Beck.

Helm Tunnel. Length of 571 yards. This tunnel, standing near a hamlet after which it is named, was driven through red marl.

Ormside Viaduct. 10 arches, 200 yards long, 90 feet high. One of the piers stands in the river Eden, which is here crossed by the railway for the first time.

Long Marton Viaduct. 5 spans, 108 yards long, 60 feet high. Crosses Trout beck, a tributary of the Eden.

Crowdundle Viaduct. 4 arches, 86 yards long, 55 feet high. The Crowdundle Beck was the old boundary between Cumberland and Westmorland.

Culgaith Tunnel. 661 yards long. Single ventilation shaft of 74 feet.

Little Salkeld Viaduct. 7 spans, 134 yards long, 60 feet high, crossing Briggle Beck.

Eden Lacy Viaduct. 7 arches, 137 yards long, 60 feet high. Spans the Eden and was constructed of the native New Red Sandstone. Normally, four of the piers rest in the river.

Lazonby Tunnel. 99 yards long. Was cut through red sandstone at a point where, originally, a cutting was intended.

Baron Wood. Two tunnels of this name, one 207 yards long, the other 251 yards long. They penetrate an area of New Red Sandstone.

Armathwaite Tunnel. 325 yards long, with a single ventilation shaft, 50 feet deep.

Armathwaite Viaduct. 9 arches, 176 yards long, 80 feet maximum height. A slightly curved structure.

For Further Reading

(A selected list in order of publication)

The Midland Railway: Its Rise and Progress, Frederick S. Williams (1876).

The Story of the Settle - Carlisle Line, Frederick W. Houghton & W. Hubert Foster (Norman Arch, 1948).

North of Leeds: The Leeds-Settle-Carlisle Line and its Branches, Peter E. Baughan (Roundhouse, 1966).

Rails in the Fells, David Jenkinson (Peco, 1973).

Seven Years Hard: Building the Settle - Carlisle Railway, W. R. Mitchell & N. J. Mussett (Dalesman, 1976).

Dales Rail: A report of an experimental project in the Yorkshire Dales National Park (Countryside Commission, 1979).

Ganger, Guard and Signalman: Working Memories of the Settle & Carlisle, Dick Fawcett (Bradford Barton, 1981).

A Regional History of the Railways of Great Britain: The Lake Counties David Joy (David & Charles, 1983).

Settle – Carlisle in Colour, David Joy (Dalesman, 1983).

The Wensleydale Railway, C.S. Hallas (Dalesman, 1984).

Life on the Settle – Carlisle Railway: Anecdotes collected from railwaymen and their families, W.R. Mitchell (Dalesman, 1984).

The Settle and Carlisle Railway: Summary Report (PEIDA, 1984).

Portrait of the Settle – Carlisle, David Joy (Dalesman, 1984).

Interpreting the heritage of the Settle – Carlisle railway line, Centre for Environmental Interpretation, Manchester Polytechnic (Countryside Commission, 1985).

Men of the Settle – Carlisle, W.R. Mitchell (Dalesman, 1985).

Retraining Settle – Carlisle: a report for the Joint Action Committee (TEST, 1986).

To Kill a Railway: The run-down of the Settle – Carlisle line, Stan Abbot (Leading Edge, 1986).

Stations and Structures of the Settle & Carlisle Railway, V.R. Anderson & G.K. Fox (Oxford Publishing, 1986).